Eating & Drinking on the Open Road

•

"...an opinionated little compendium."
~ New York Times

"...irresistible little guide."
~ Chicago Tribune

"an elegant, small guide..."
~ Minneapolis Star Tribune

""...a terrific primer for first-time visitors."
~ Houston Chronicle

*""...opening up the world of good eating with their
innovative paperback series."*
~ Salt Lake Tribune

"...travelers who know their cervelle *(brains) from*
cervelle de canut *(herbed cheese spread)."*
~ USA Today

**OPEN ROAD TRAVEL GUIDES – YOUR GUIDES
TO PLANET EARTH!**

Whether you're going abroad or planning a trip to the United
States, take Open Road along on your journey. Our books have
been praised by **Travel & Leisure**, **The Los Angeles Times**,
Newsday, **Booklist**, **US News & World Report**, **Endless
Vacation**, **American Bookseller**, **Coast to Coast** and many
other magazines and newspapers!

Don't just see the world - experience it with Open Road!

ABOUT THE AUTHORS

Michael Dillon is a graphic designer. Andy Herbach is a lawyer. Both authors reside in Milwaukee, Wisconsin. They are the authors of *Eating and Drinking in Paris*, *Eating and Drinking in Italy*, *Eating and Drinking in Spain* and *Eating and Drinking in Latin America*.

You can e-mail comments, additions and corrections through www.eatndrink.com.

OPEN ROAD –
TRAVEL GUIDES TO PLANET EARTH!

Open Road Publishing has guide books to exciting, fun destinations on four continents. As veteran travelers, our goal is to bring you the best travel guides available anywhere!

No small task, but here's what we offer:

- All Open Road travel guides are written by authors with a distinct, opinionated point of view – not some sterile committee or team of writers. Our authors are experts in the areas covered and are polished writers.

- Our guides are geared to people who want to make their own travel choices. We'll show you how to discover the real destination – not just see some place from a tour bus window.

- We're strong on the basics, but we also provide terrific choices for those looking to get off the beaten path and experience the country or city – not just see it or pass through it.

- We give you the best, but we also tell you about the worst and what to avoid. Nobody should waste his or her time and money on their hard-earned vacation because of bad or inadequate travel advice.

- Our guides assume nothing. We tell you everything you need to know to have the trip of a lifetime – presented in a fun, literate, no-nonsense style.

- And, above all, we welcome your input, ideas, and suggestions to help us put out the best travel guides possible.

EATING AND DRINKING IN

Paris

•

Menu Reader and Restaurant Guide

Andy Herbach and Michael Dillon

OPEN ROAD PUBLISHING

Second edition

Copyright © 2004 by Andy Herbach and Michael Dillon
- All Rights Reserved -

Cover design and illustration by Michael Dillon
Back cover photo by Elizabeth Enslen Dillon

Library of Congress Control No. 2003117067
ISBN 1-59360-015-1

Contents

EATING AND DRINKING IN PARIS

AN INTRODUCTION

When you think of Paris, you may think of the Eiffel Tower, the Louvre or the Champs-Elysées. When we think of Paris, the first thing that comes to our mind is food.

Of course, every traveler has a different set of desires and expectations: rest and relaxation, shopping, exploring, hiking, reading...whatever. For us, the making of a memorable vacation begins and ends with food. Not that we don't like and appreciate museums, gardens, shopping – okay, we hate shopping – but we do enjoy jogging along the Seine and doing normal tourist things like exploring medieval churches. And sure, the Louvre is great, but have you had one of those long, skinny French hot dogs the vendors sell on the streets outside? Honestly, we can't remember if we saw the Mona Lisa, but that hot dog, covered with shredded Swiss cheese, grilled golden brown and then slathered with Dijon mustard, was exquisite and remains a cherished memory of a visit to Paris.

Beyond the simple pleasures of eating, dining in a foreign country gives you an insight into the soul of its people. It's a glimpse of their customs, their likes and dislikes, their foibles, their accomplishments. It puts you in contact with local culture. In fact, for most travelers, the closest they will come to actually interacting with real live natives is when they are eating in a restaurant and speaking to waiters and bartenders. While we probably wouldn't count them as close friends, there are waiters who remember us and who have made our meals more enjoyable simply through their personal interactions with us.

If you love to travel as we do, you know the importance of a good guide. Dining, like traveling, requires the same. A good guide can make the difference between a memorable evening and a nightmare or maybe just a dull one, but who wants a dull evening when they're on vacation? There is nothing worse than hiking all over a city looking for a good place to eat dinner, finding nothing, in near panic settling for whatever comes along next, having a lousy meal, then, upon leaving, discovering what looks like the best restaurant in the world right around the corner. Believe us, it happens all the time. The restaurant-guide portion of our book is a quick list of some of our favorite places in Paris, and the menu-reader section will help you find your way around a menu written in French. It gives you the freedom to fearlessly enter places you might never have entered before and order a dinner without shouting, pointing, or hand waving. This book also contains an alphabetical listing of food and drink commonly found on menus in Paris.

Eating & Drinking in Paris isn't so much about food and wine. It's really about easing the process of ordering food and having a good time – or at least not a stressful time – doing it. Our guide was created for the not-so-daring traveler who wants to enjoy and experience authentic cuisine and know what he or she is eating.

OUR MISSION

As silly as it might sound, we have one:

No Menus in English.

Aside from, say, in England.

We want people to eat in restaurants without English menus. We don't like to see the United States when we're visiting France; we want foreign when we're on foreign soil. When we visited Athens we were horrified to see a gigantic neon-and-plastic, two-story Kenny Rogers Roast Chicken franchise on Syntagma Square right smack across from the Greek Parliament. On the beautiful port of Marigot on the island of St. Martin in the French West Indies, a single Kentucky Fried Chicken put all of the small, locally owned and picturesque grill shacks, called *lolos*, out of business, virtually destroying what was charming about the port. We have nothing against fast food, but when we're in France, we want it to look French. We don't want to see the golden arches under the Eiffel Tower (they tried to do that...seriously) and we don't want to see a menu in English. As we see it, a menu in English is the first step in the Americanization of the restaurants of the world, the first domino. And once it's not foreign, what's the point of going?

ABOUT EATING AND DRINKING IN PARIS

No other city in the world has a greater number of places to eat per square mile than Paris. Nowhere else can you find the variety, the charm, the sheer joy and celebration of food. And nowhere else can you be more intimidated trying to get fed. Parisians observe all kinds of decorum about their food. They have many, many types of eating establishments which to us are confusing. What's wrong with calling them all restaurants? They eat in a nearly ritualistic manner and want you to do so as well. As Americans we feel we are often blundering into a private party and haven't received all the pertinent information. The following is some of that information.

THE MENU A menu is a fixed-price meal, not that piece of paper listing the food items. If you want what we consider a menu, you need to ask for *la carte*. The menu is almost always posted on the front of the restaurant so you know what you're getting into, both foodwise and pricewise, before you enter. The fixed-price daily menu (*menu fixe*) will generally include several choices for each of 2 or 3 courses. The daily fixed-price menu is cheaper than ordering off the menu (*carte*). Our American term *à la carte* means 'of the menu,' in case you hadn't noticed.

Restaurants frequently offer a plate of the day (*plat du jour*), and some restaurants offer a set-price gourmet menu (*menu dégustation*) of specialties of the chef. The price of a meal will occasionally include the house wine (*vin compris*).

A simple green salad (*salade verte*) is occasionally served with or sometimes after the main course, before the cheese course or dessert. Rarely is this type of salad even listed on the menu. Larger, more involved, and to us what seem like full meals, salads such as *roquefort*, *lardons* and *endive* are usually listed as first courses or *entrées*. However, times have changed and you may now order a green salad as an appetizer but you will most likely have to ask for it, because, as we said earlier, you won't find it on the menu.

An *entrée* is a first course, the *plat* is the main course, followed by cheese and then dessert. Coffee is served at the end – never with your meal. There are all sorts of coffees that you can order decaffeinated which, if your meal is ending at midnight, as so often happens in Paris, you might want to consider. Ask for *déca* which rhymes with day-cah. You'll find a list of the different types of coffees on page 62.

WHY IS THERE A DOG AT THE TABLE NEXT TO ME? Parisians really love their dogs. It is not uncommon (no matter what type of eating establishment you are dining in) to find several dogs under tables, or even on their own chairs.

ASKING FOR YOUR BILL The bill in a restaurant is called *l'addition*...but the bill in a bar is called *le compte* or *la note*; confusing? It's easier if you just make a scribbling motion with your fingers on the palm of your hand.

TIPPING A service charge is almost always added to your bill in Paris. Depending on the service, it is sometimes appropriate to leave

an additional 5 to 10%. The menu will usually note that service is included (*service compris*). Sometimes this is abbreviated with the letters s.c. The letters s.n.c. stand for *service non compris*; this means that the service is not included in the price, and you must leave a tip.

You will sometimes find *couvert* or cover charge on your menu (a small charge just for placing your butt at the table).

MEALTIMES In Paris, lunch is served from noon to around 2:00 p.m., and dinner from 8:00 p.m. to 11:00 p.m. Restaurants usually have two seatings: at 8:00 or 8:30 p.m., and at 10:00 or 10:30 p.m. The restaurant will be less crowded at the early seating, but don't worry, it will fill up fast. There also tends to be less cigarette smoke early in the evening, before the place gets packed with people.

RESERVATIONS It's advisable if you're visiting a restaurant (as opposed to a *bistro* or *café*) to have reservations. Although you might see an empty restaurant and assume there will be seats available, most places we have listed will be full by 8:00 p.m. – with people who have made reservations. We advise making reservations in person. We like to do a walk-by in the afternoon, stop in and make reservations. Don't be afraid. The word for reservation is the same in English and French. You can do times and numbers with your fingers. If you speak a little French, you can do it on the phone. The problem with phoning, however, comes when, after you've said in a timid voice that you would like to make reservations if possible, they ask you a question in rapid-fire French and at that pace asking what your name is sounds pretty much like how many people are in the party or what time were you thinking about eating. Be patient; eventually you'll get the idea across.

WATER Europeans joke that you can tell a U.S. tourist from his "fanny pack," clothes and ubiquitous bottle of mineral water. Tap water is safe in Paris. Occasionally, you will find *non potable* signs in restrooms. This means that the water is not safe for drinking.

Waiters and waitresses often bring *eau minérale* (mineral water) to your table. You will be charged for it, so if you don't want mineral water ask for *une carafe d'eau* or *eau du robinet* (tap water).

WHAT TO DO WHEN NOTHING SEEMS TO BE OPEN Sundays can be frustrating. Nothing seems to be open. You can phone in advance but that isn't necessarily going to work because the place might not be open when you call. The best thing to do is to go to an area where there is a high concentration of restaurants. We have some of them listed on page 15.

We think of most of these places as restaurants. We have a hard time
seeing the differences between many of these establishments. Cafés
seem like bars, bistros seem like brasseries, and they all seem like
restaurants. What some people think of as a limited menu can seem
complete to someone else (like us). Our full list of restaurants starting
on page 19 includes cafés, brasseries, bistros and restaurants.

Alimentation: A small food store.
Auberge: An inn serving food and drink. These are most often found
in the country, but restaurants in Paris also use the name. One
favorite is Auberge Pyrénnées-Cévennes (see the restaurant section).
Bar à café: Coffee shop serving light meals. Don't be misled by the
name, though, as they rarely serve alcohol.
Bistro: Smaller and less fashionable than a restaurant, serving tradi-
tional, simple French food. Some are very similar to taverns or pubs.
Bar à champagne: Champagne bar.
Bar à vin: Wine bar.
Boucherie: Butcher's shop.
Boulangerie: Bakery. Nowhere else on earth can you get *baguettes*
that taste like they do in France. Bread is often offered *bien cuit*
(crusty) or *bien tendre* (doughy). Many *boulangeries* also sell
sandwiches, tarts, quiches and small pizzas.
Brasserie: Originally, this term referred to a beer hall, but today
serves food and drink.
Buffet: Eating establishment usually found in railroad stations.
Cabaret: Dinner and a show.
Café: Simple café dining is one of the pleasures of a trip to Paris. You
can learn more sitting in a café for an hour than spending the day in a
museum. In Paris, people-watching is like no other place in the
world. Cafés serve alcoholic beverages and snacks. Some serve
complete meals.
Cave: Cellar. This also refers to a wine shop. See Vins et Alcools.
Charcuteries: Originally these were pork butchers selling pork, ham,
sausages, *jambon de Paris* and sometimes chicken. Now, most are
delicatessens with prepared salads, quiches and other food tarts.
Chevaline: Horse-meat butcher's shop. These shops are becoming
few and far between, but have a small and devoted clientele. Usually,
there is a horse-head emblem on the front of the shop.
Chocolaterie: Chocolate shop.
Confiserie: Sweet shop.

Crémerie: Cream (and cheese) shop.
Crêperies: Popular for lunch, serving *crêpes* (filled thin pancakes).

Ti Jos
14th/Métro Vavin
30 rue Delambre
01/43.22.57.69
Closed Tues. (dinner), weekends & part of Aug.
Popular *crêperie* featuring *crêpes* and other specialties of
Brittany.
Inexpensive

Emporter: Carry-out foods.
Épicerie: Grocer's shop (literally "spice shop").
Express: Any establishment with this name is usually a snack bar.
Fromagerie: Serves up to 400 official types of cheese.
Glaces et Sorbets/Glacier: Ice cream & sorbet shop. The best-known
ice cream shop in Paris is **Berthillon**, on the Île St-Louis, 4th/Métro
Pont-Marie, 31 rue Saint-Louis-en-I'lle, 01/43.54.31.61.
Hostellerie: Upscale country restaurant.
Marché: Market.
Marchand de Légumes: Vegetable shop.
Pâtisseries: Pastry shops. The Parisian favorite of *baba au rhum*
(spongecake soaked in rum) was invented at **Stohrer**, 2nd/Métro Les
Halles, 51 rue Montorgueil, 01/42.33.38.20, Closed part of Aug.
Pizzerias: You can figure this one out yourself.
Poissonnerie: Seafood shop.
Relais: Country inn or restaurant.
Restaurant: See our separate section on recommended restaurants.
Restoroute: Restaurant found on the highway.
Rôtisserie: Restaurant that usually specializes in roasted and grilled
meats, especially chicken.
Salon de Thé: Open mid-morning to late evening, serving light fare,
salads, cakes, ice cream and, of course, *thé* (tea).
Tabac: Bars where you can also buy cigarettes (they are, in fact, the
only places in France where you can buy tobacco), stamps, tickets for
public transportation, lottery tickets and phone cards. They are often
also *cafés*.
Traiteur: Delicatessen (this can also mean caterer). There seem to be
Indo-Chinese and Italian traiteurs all over the place. The food is usually good and inexpensive.

Triperie: Tripe shop.
Vins et Alcools: Wine and liquor shop.
Volailler: Poultry shop.

~~ A FEW NOTES ABOUT USING THIS GUIDE ~~

Even people who speak passable French can have trouble reading a menu. The grand-sounding *suprême de volaille* is simply a chicken breast. *Cervelle* is brains, but *cervelle de canut* is an herbed cheese spread from Lyon.

Remember that the dish that you ordered may not be exactly as described in this guide. Every chef is (and should be) innovative. What we have listed for you in this guide is the most common version of a dish.

Times can change and restaurants can close, so do a walk-by earlier in the day or the day before, if possible.

Each of our recommended restaurants offers something different. Some have great food and little ambiance. Others have great ambiance and adequate food. Still others have both. Our goal is to find restaurants that are moderately priced and enjoyable. All restaurants have been tried and tested. Not enough can be said for a friendly welcome and great service. No matter how fabulous the meal, the experience will always be better when the staff treats you as if they actually want you there rather than simply tolerating your presence.

Be careful, menus in English are often wrong.

TIPS FOR BUDGET DINING IN PARIS There is no need to spend a lot of money in Paris to have good food. Of course it helps when the euro is weaker than the dollar, but there are all kinds of fabulous foods to be had inexpensively all over Paris.

Eat at a neighborhood restaurant or bistro. You'll always know the price of a meal before entering, as almost all Paris restaurants post the menu and prices in the window. Never order anything whose price is not known in advance. If you see *selon grosseur* (sometimes abbreviated as s/g) this means that you are paying by weight, which can be extremely expensive.

Delis, *traiteurs* and food stores can provide cheap and wonderful meals. Buy some cheese, bread, wine and other snacks and have a picnic in one of Paris's great parks. In fact, no matter what, you should go into a *boulangerie* and buy a *baguette* at least once. Remember to pack a corkscrew and eating utensils when you leave home.

Lunch, even at the most expensive restaurants listed in this guide, always has a lower fixed price. So, have lunch as your main meal.

Restaurants and bistros that have menus written in English (especially those near tourist attractions) are almost always more expensive than neighborhood restaurants and bistros.

Large department stores frequently have supermarkets in the basement and restaurants that have reasonably priced food. **La Samaritaine** (1st/Métro Pont Neuf, 19 rue de la Monnaie) has a supermarket and a reasonably priced café on the 10th floor. Even if you don't eat there, you can take the elevator to the 9th floor and the steps to the 10th and treat yourself to a great free view of the Paris skyline. It's interesting to visit a supermarket like Monoprix, where, usually, there's barely a snack-food section to speak of, if one at all. Not at all like at home!

Street vendors generally sell inexpensive and terrific food; you'll find excellent hot dogs, *crêpes* and roast-chicken sandwiches all over Paris. At lunch time, you'll see Parisians eating long, thin *baguettes* filled with chicken, mayonnaise and sliced eggs throughout the city.

For the cost of a cup of coffee or a drink, you can linger at a café and watch the world pass you by for as long as you want. It's one of Paris's greatest bargains.

Kids seem to love **Hippopotamus**, a chain of inexpensive restaurants with over twenty locations in Paris. The restaurants have noisy televisions everywhere, paper table covers for coloring (they provide the crayons) and balloons (everything you thought you left behind at home). *Paris With Kids* is a good source for travel with children.

And don't eat at McDonald's, for God's sake.

FOOD MARKETS AND OTHER PLACES TO FIND FOOD

If nothing else, food markets are very interesting. Though you may feel intimidated by the wild goings-on (not to mention the sights and smells) it is absolutely worth a trip to see a real outdoor Parisian market. Filled with colorful vendors, stinky cheese, fresh produce, poultry and hanging rabbits, this is real Paris at its most diverse and beautiful. Parisians still shop (some every day) at food markets around the city. Unless noted otherwise, all are open Tuesday through noon on Sunday. Some of the best-known are:

> Rue Montorgueil, 1st/Métro Les Halles
> Rue Mouffetard, 5th/Métro Censier-Daubenton
> Rue de Buci, 6th/Métro Mabillon
> Rue Cler, 7th/Métro École Militaire
> Marché Bastille on the boulevard Richard Lenoir,
>   11th/Métro Bastille (open Thursday and Sunday)
> Rue Daguerre, 14th/Métro Denfert-Rochereau
> Rue Poncelet, 17th/Métro Ternes

Markets are places that you might appreciate as you would a museum, but there are other places around Paris where you can also see and experience food in a unique setting. The area around the Place de la Madeleine (8th/Métro Madeleine) is packed with fabulous specialty food shops (the windows of the food store **Fauchon** are worth a trip by themselves), wine dealers, restaurants, and tea rooms. This is a perfect place for eating and purchasing culinary souvenirs. There is something for every taste – but this is an upscale area, and can be expensive. In addition to food markets and specialty shops, there are several areas in Paris where many restaurants are concentrated in small pockets. These are areas that are charming just in and of themselves, nice to walk through and nice to eat in, particularly outside on a nice evening.

One area is on rue Pot-de-Fer between la rue Tournefort and la rue Mouffetard, just off the market. It's a slip of a street but it is lined with charming restaurants with clothed tables set for dinner, colored lights hanging from the roof overhangs, and a uniquely Parisian ambiance (Métro Monge).

Uniquely Parisian is *not* the Passage Brady in the 10th arrondissement. You can enter the narrow *passage* around 33 boulevard Strasbourg and find mostly Indian, but also Turkish and Moroccan, restaurants in an interestingly Indian setting. These are inexpensive restaurants in a working-class neighborhood, and the passage, while exotic in many ways, is not upscale (Métro Château d'Eau).

There are several restaurants and bars on the lovely Place Sainte-Catherine (between la rue Malher and la rue de Sévigné) in the Marais, 4th. There are many restaurants in this neighborhood in general, but the Place Sainte-Catherine is a special, quiet respite in this newly fashionable area (Métro Saint-Paul).

You'll find loads of restaurants off of la rue Saint-Jacques in the area around la rue Saint-Séverin and la rue de la Huchette in the 5th. This area, a short walk from Notre Dame, is filled with French, Italian, Greek and other restaurants jammed into small streets. It's a very pleasant walk, and you're bound to find somewhere to eat. Nearby in the 6th is the cour du Commerce, a tiny alleyway off of la rue St-André-des-Arts, which is lined with restaurants to fit all pocketbooks (Métros Saint-Michel, Odéon or Cluny-La Sorbonne).

TEN SIMPLE RULES

OF DINING IN PARIS

---

1. Avoid eating in a restaurant that has a menu written in English. In case you haven't gathered, we're against them for a number of reasons. One good reason is that at one restaurant, we were automatically given the English menu (which is really irritating, since we hate being so obviously American) and we discovered as we walked out that it bore no relationship to the French menu which was more than twice as long.

2. Don't be afraid. They can't and won't hurt you. They are not laughing at you, they don't dislike you, they aren't even thinking about you. Waiters in France are trained professionals whose job is to serve you. Despite what you've heard, they want you to have a good time. Sometimes they are just mystified by what we do.

When asked what the French think about Thanksgiving Julia Child replied, "The French aren't thinking about Thanksgiving, they're focused on themselves." Which pretty much sums it up.

3. Don't ever call the waiter "*garçon*." Though sometimes in bars a Parisian will use this word, travelers should never use it.

4. Try to make reservations. This isn't as difficult as it seems; the words are similar in both languages and they'll get the gist of what you're trying to do. We often do a walk by in the afternoon and stop in to make the reservation. When we go back that night they are almost always happy to see us again.

5. Return to a restaurant if you like it. If you have the luxury of time and can withstand the temptation to try other restaurants, you will always be treated better if they recognize you. Few travelers return to the same restaurant.

6. Parisians dine leisurely. Don't expect to get the same speed of service as at home. For the French, dinner is nearly a ritual. In its full-blown form, it begins with an *apéritif*. This is often accompanied

by an *amuse-gueule*, a little snack of some sort. After this, you order an *hors-d'oeuvre*. Then comes an *entrée*, which is a first course – *pâté* or a composed salad, such as a salad with shrimp or hard-boiled eggs – and then the main course which will most likely be meat or fish. The main course is sometimes accompanied by or followed by a salad, but it is a simple green salad. After this, just when you think you will explode and have secretly unbuckled your belt, the *serveur* arrives with selections from the cheese platter that are followed by dessert, and, finally, coffee. But if you do not want to follow the French protocol, don't. Even if the waiter seems to disapprove, do what you like.

7. Don't talk loudly. You will notice that the French speak softly, Americans don't; we just can't help it. But believe us: those loud voices coupled with running shoes, backpacks, "fanny packs," large, conspicuous guide books and cameras are like wearing a neon sign announcing that you are a tourist, an American tourist.

8. Stand your ground without being aggressive. In the years we've been traveling, it seems that waiters have become more relaxed about the rituals of eating, and will accommodate you if you insist on what you want – within reason, of course.

9. Visit a street vendor at least once in Paris. Whether it's sandwiches, hot dogs or *crêpes*, Parisian street vendors sell delicious "food on the run." Do yourself a favor, and sample some.

10. Always be courteous. Remember that you are a guest in their country. There are simple things that the French do that we don't, like excusing yourself or saying please all the time.

S'il vous plaît (seel voo play) after nearly everything is a safe way to be very polite. Seriously. A polite Parisian ALWAYS finishes a greeting (such as *bonjour* – hello) or affirmation (such as *oui* – yes) with a title. Thus, *bonjour* is always *bonjour, madame* or *m'sieur* and yes or no is always *oui, m'sieur* or *madame.* And just so you know, you say *bonjour*, which is essentially hello, all day and night. *Bonsoir* – good evening – is reserved for leaving and after 7:00 p.m., and *bonne nuit* – good night – is only used when you are actually on your way to bed.

PLACES TO EAT

RESTAURANTS, BISTROS, BRASSERIES
CAFÉS AND SALONS DE THÉ

Phone numbers, days closed and hours of operation often change, so it's advisable to check ahead. Restaurants in tourist areas may have different hours and days of operation during low season. Reservations are recommended for all restaurants unless noted. The telephone country code for France is 33. When calling within France you must dial the area code. The area code for Paris is 01. However, you do not use the 0 before the area code when calling France from the USA or Canada. Confused?

Oui m'sieur?
Combien de personnes?

Here's what it looks like:

From the United States:
(011) 33 1/43.26.48.23

From within Paris:
01/43.26.48.23

Prices are for a main course and without wine.
Lunch, even at the most expensive restaurants listed below, always has a lower fixed price. Credit cards accepted unless noted.

Inexpensive: under $10
Moderate: $11 - $20
Expensive: $21 - $30
Very Expensive: over $30

Allard ✓

6th/Métro Odéon
41 rue St-André-des-Arts
01/43.26.48.23
fax 01/46.33.04.02
Closed Sun. & part of Aug.
Diners repeatedly praise the service
and food at this typical Parisian bistro.
Moderate

In our restaurant recommendations, the first line indicates the arrondissement (district) and the closest métro stop.

Auberge Pyrénnées-Cévennes

11th/Métro République
106 rue de la Folie-Méricourt
01/43.57.33.78
Closed Sat. (lunch) & Sun.
Small, charming restaurant serving the food of Southwest France.
Hams hanging from the ceiling add to the charm. Try the *cassoulet*.
Moderate

L'Avant Goût

13th/Métro Place d'Italie
26 rue Bobillot
01/53.80.24.00
fax 01/53.80.00.77
Closed Sun., Mon. & most of Aug.

Brioche.

Mix with the French in this small, crowded bistro near the place
d'Italie. Consistently good cuisine and very French. Try the *pot-au-feu* (stew of meat and vegetables).
Inexpensive - Moderate

Baracane

4th/Métro Bastille
38 rue des Tournelles
01/42.71.43.33
Closed Sat. (lunch) & Sun.
Small restaurant in the Marais featuring the specialties
of Southwest France (especially *confit*).
Inexpensive - Moderate

Au Bascou
3rd/Métro Arts-et-Métiers
38 rue Réaumur
01/42.72.69.25
fax 01/42.72.69.25
Closed Sat. (lunch), Sun., Mon. (lunch) & Aug.
Modern bistro near the place de la République serving
Basque specialties. *Piperade* (a spicy omelet) is the specialty.
Moderate

Bernardaud
8th/Métro Concorde
8 bis Galerie Royale (11 rue Royale)
01/42.66.22.55
fax 01/47.42.60.06
Closed Sun.
Fancy and fashionable tea room.
Moderate

Bistro 121
15th/Métro Boucicaut
121 rue de la Convention
01/45.57.52.90
fax 01/45.57.14.69
Occasionally closed on Mon.
A favorite of many seeking a romantic, elegant evening in a classic
French bistro. Try the *poulet fermier* (free-range chicken).
Moderate

Bistro des Deux Théâtres
9th/Métro Trinité
18 rue Blanche
01/45.26.41.43
fax 01/48.74.08.92
Affordable dining at this neighborhood bistro near the place de
Clichy.
Moderate

Bofinger
4th/Métro Bastille
5 rue de la Bastille
01/42.72.87.82
fax 01/42.72.97.68
Open until 1 a.m.
Beautiful glass-roofed brasserie with lots of stained glass and brass, located between the place des Vosges and the place de la Bastille. It's the oldest Alsatian brasserie in Paris, and still serves traditional dishes like *choucroute* (sauerkraut) and large platters of shellfish. Across the street and less expensive is **Le Petit Bofinger**, 6 rue de la Bastille,
01/42.72.05.23.
Moderate

Les Bouchons de François Clerc
5th/Métro Maubert-Mutualité
12 rue Hôtel Colbert
01/43.54.15.34
fax 01/46.34.68.07
Closed Sat. (lunch) & Sun.
Our French editor recommended this restaurant and everyone we've sent there has loved it (especially the cheese course and reasonably priced wines). There are also restaurants at:
8th/Métro Alma-Marceau, 7 rue du Boccador, 01/47.23.57.80,
8th/Métro Charles-de-Gaulle-Étoile, 6 rue Arsène Houssaye,
01/42.89.15.51 and 17th/Métro Villiers, 22 rue de la Terrasse
01/42.27.31.51.
Moderate

Bouillon Racine ✓

Beautiful Restaurant!

6th/Métro Cluny-La Sorbonne or Odéon
3 rue Racine
01/44.32.15.60
fax 01/44.32.15.61
Popular brasserie serving Belgian cuisine in a historic building. Try the *waterzooi*. They also offer a large vegetarian plate.
Moderate

La Boulangerie
20th/Métro Ménilmontant
15 rue des Panoyaux
01/43.58.45.45
Closed Sat. (lunch) and Sun.
A classic French bistro with a beautiful mosaic floor in a former
bakery in the Ménilmontant area near Père-Lachaise cemetery.
Moderate

Brasserie Balzar
5th/Métro Odéon
49 rue des Ecoles
01/43.54.13.67
fax 01/44.07.14.91
This Latin Quarter brasserie opened in 1898 and serves traditional
French cuisine. It's known for its roast chicken, onion soup and
"colorful" waiters.
Moderate

Brasserie Flo
10th/Métro Château d'Eau
7 cour des Petites-Écuries (enter from 63 rue du Fg-St-Denis)
01/47.70.13.59
fax 01/42.47.00.80
Open daily until 1:30 a.m.
Alsatian food and Parisian atmosphere at this 1886 brasserie, on a
passageway in an area not frequented by tourists. Jam-packed with
some of the strangest people you will see in Paris, and getting there is
half the fun.
Moderate

Café Beaubourg
4th/Métro Hôtel de Ville
100 rue Saint-Martin
01/48.87.63.96
Looking onto the Centre Pompidou and packed with an artsy crowd.
Recommended for a drink and perhaps a snack. The food is not that
great, but the bathrooms are worth the trip.
Moderate

Café de Flore
6th/Métro Saint-Germain-des-Prés
172 boulevard. Saint-Germain-des-Prés
01/45.48.55.26
Another famous café and a favorite of tourists and Parisians
alike (next door to Les Deux Magots). At the moment,
Café de Flore is in fashion with Parisians and Les Deux
Magots is not. Why? We're not sure. They look the same to us.
Moderate

Café de la Paix
9th/Métro Opéra
12 boulevard des Capucines (place de l'Opéra)
01/40.07.30.20
Famous café (not really known for its food). Popular with tourists.
Another spot for outdoor people-watching (and the inside
is beautiful).
Moderate - Expensive

Café de l'Industrie
11th/Métro Bastille
16 rue St-Sabin
01/47.00.13.53
Near the Opéra Bastille, this inexpensive café features a limited
menu, a diverse wine list and an artsy crowd.
Inexpensive

Café du Passage
11th/Métro Bastille (a few blocks from the Place de la Bastille)
12 rue de Charonne
01/49.29.97.64
fax 01/47.00.14.00
Open daily in the evenings & Sat. at noon.
French wines and wines from around the world are available along
with reasonably priced dishes.
Moderate

Café Les Deux Magots
6th/Métro Saint-Germain-des-Prés
6 place Saint-Germain-des-Prés
01/45.48.55.25
If you're a tourist, you'll fit right in at one of Hemingway's
favorite spots. We don't really recommend that you eat here
(there is a limited menu), but have a drink and enjoy the
great people-watching.
Moderate

Café L'Été en Pente Douce
18th/Métro Château-Rouge
23 rue Muller
01/42.64.02.67

*L'été en pente
douce ~ Summer
on a gentle slope.*

Interesting and picturesque café near Sacré-Coeur where we met
Loralyn, our favorite former Parisienne. Take a break here before you
climb the steps to Sacré-Coeur!
Inexpensive

Café Marly
1st/Métro Musée du Louvre/Palais-Royal
93 rue de Rivoli
01/49.26.06.60
This café overlooks the pyramid at the
Louvre, and is popular with visitors
to the museum. The setting makes up for
any complaints about the "ordinary" food.
Moderate

*We LoVE the
pyramids.*

La Cave Gourmande
19th/Métro Danube or Botzaris
10 rue du Général-Brunet
01/40.40.03.30. Also fax
Closed Sun., Mon. & Aug.
Raves for chef Mark Singer's cuisine, but not for the trip out to this
"remote" part of Paris. "Foodies" love this place.
Moderate - Expensive

Chardenoux

A bit out of the way but worth the trip.

11th/Métro Charonne
1 rue Jules-Vallès and 23 rue Chanzy
01/43.71.49.52
fax 01/45.62.04.07
Traditional Parisian cooking in the Bastille/République. This small and friendly restaurant has been in business for almost 100 years.
Moderate

Chartier

9th/Métro rue Montmartre
7 rue du Faubourg-Montmartre
01/47.70.86.29
No reservations
Traditional Paris soup kitchen with affordable prices. The *tripes à la mode de Caen* is a frequent special of the day (we passed on that). Lots of tourists, and you may be seated with strangers which we really enjoy; it's a great way to meet people. Expect to wait in line.
Inexpensive

Chez Jenny

3rd/Métro République
39 boulevard du Temple
01/44.54.39.00
A little bit of the Alsace region of France can be found in this brasserie on the place de la République. Hope you like *choucroute* (sauerkraut).
Moderate

Chez Maître Paul

6th/Métro Odéon
12 rue Monsieur-le-Prince
01/43.54.74.59
fax 01/46.34.58.33
Closed Aug.
Hearty cooking of the Jura Mountains and Franche-Comté regions of France (near the Swiss border), which are known for their game and trout dishes.
Moderate

26

Chez Marianne
4th/Métro Saint-Paul
2 rue des Hospitalières-St-Gervais
01/42.72.18.86
Popular, charming take-away deli (you can also eat here) known for
its authentic Jewish and Eastern European specialties.
Inexpensive

Chez Paul

One of our all-time favorites!

11th/Métro Bastille
13 rue de Charonne
01/47.00.34.57
Our favorite bistro in Paris. Never a bad meal (try the rabbit), and ask
to eat upstairs. The service can be very Parisian, if you know what we
mean.
Moderate

La Closerie des Lilas
14th/Métro Raspail/Vavin
171 boulevard du Montparnasse
01/40.51.34.50
Lenin and Trotsky are among the few who have visited this historic
café. There is a terrace, piano bar, brasserie (moderate) and
restaurant (expensive).
Moderate - Expensive

La Coupole
14th/Métro Vavin
102 boulevard Montparnasse
01/43.20.14.20
fax 01/43.35.46.14
A Montparnasse institution since the days of Picasso, this noisy
brasserie is a favorite among tourists. It's known for its oysters. The
atmosphere is "belle époque."
Moderate

Le Dix Vin
15th/Métro Pasteur
57 rue Falguière
01/43.20.91.77
Closed Sun. & Mon.
No credit cards
Neighborhood wine bar with solid, reasonably priced food and wine.
You'll find traditional Parisian bistro fare served by attentive waiters
in an area not frequented by most tourists.
Moderate

L'Ecluse
11th/Métro Bastille
13 rue de la Roquette
01/48.05.19.12
Chain of trendy wine bars. Not the greatest food in Paris, but great
for wine tasting (especially Bordeaux). You come here to taste the
selection of wines by the glass and have a light meal such as *charcuterie assortie* (assorted cold meats). Other locations are in the 6th at
15 quai des Grands-Augustins (Métro St-Michel), in the 17th at 1
rue d'Armaillé (Métro Charles de Gaulle-Étoile), in the 8th at 15
place de la Madeleine (Métro Madeleine), in the 8th at 64 rue
François 1er (Métro George V), and in the 1st at 34 place du Marché
St-Honoré (Métro Tuileries).
Moderate

L'Enoteca
4th/Métro Saint-Paul
25 rue Charles V
01/42.78.91.44
fax 01/44.59.31.72
Attractive Italian wine bar/bistro in the Marais.
It has one of the largest Italian wine
selections in Paris.
Moderate

These restaurants are very expensive and highly praised. You will find them in nearly every other guide book. Reservations well in advance are a must, as are jacket and tie.

Alain Ducasse
Restaurant Plaza Athénée
8th/Métro Alma-Marceau
25 avenue Montaigne
01/53.67.65.00
fax 01/53.67.65.12
www.alain-ducasse.com

L'Ambroisie
4th/Métro St-Paul
9 place des Vosges
01/42.78.51.45 (also fax)

L'Arpège
7th/Métro Varenne
84 rue de Varenne
01/47.05.09.06
fax 01/44.18.98.39
www.alain-passard.com

Le Grand Véfour
1st/Métro Palais-Royal
17 rue Beaujolais
01/42.96.56.27
fax 01/42.86.80.71

Guy Savoy
17th/Métro Charles-de-Gaulle-Étoile or Ternes
18 rue Troyon
01/43.80.40.61
fax 01/46.22.43.09
www.guysavoy.com

Jules Verne
7th/Métro Bir-Hakeim
Second level of the Eiffel Tower
01/45.55.61.44
fax 01/47.05.29.41
www.tour-eiffel.fr

Lucas-Carton
8th/Métro Madeleine
9 place de la Madeleine
01/42.65.22.90
fax 01/42.65.06.23
www.lucascarton.com

Pierre Gagnaire
8th/Métro George V
6 rue Balzac (Hôtel Balzac)
01/58.36.12.50
fax 01/58.36.12.51
www.pierre-gagnaire.com

Taillevent
8th/Métro Charles-de-Gaulle-Étoile or George V
15 rue Lamennais
01/44.95.15.01
fax 01/42.25.95.18
www.taillevent.com

La Tour d'Argent
5th/Métro Maubert
15 quai de la Tournelle
01/43.54.23.31
fax 01/44.07.12.04
www.latourdargent.com

L'Atelier de Joël Robuchon
7th/Métro Rue du Bac
5 rue de Montalembert
01/42.22.56.56 (no reservations)

La Fontaine de Mars
7th/Métro Ecole-Militaire
129 rue St-Dominique
01/47.05.46.44
fax 01/47.05.11.13
Red-checked tablecloths, friendly service and reasonable prices near
the Eiffel Tower. Try the *poulet fermier aux morilles* (free-range
chicken with morel mushrooms). Next door is **L'Auvergne
Gourmande** for group dining.
Moderate

Le Flamboyant
14th/Métro Pernety
11 rue Boyer-Barret
01/45.41.00.22
Closed Sun. & Mon.
If you're a fan of Caribbean food, this is a great French West
Indian restaurant, though it's a bit of a trip.
Inexpensive

Au Gamin de Paris
4th/Métro Saint-Paul
51 rue Vieille du Temple
01/42.78.97.24

Small Marais bar/restaurant serving Parisian specialties.
We've never had a bad meal here.
Moderate

Jo Goldenberg
4th/Métro Saint-Paul
7 rue des Rosiers
01/48.87.20.16
fax 01/42.78.15.29

*Jo Goldenberg
is a favorite.
Definitely an
experience.*

Jewish deli in the Marais that became more famous for the wrong
reason (the bombing by anti-Semitic terrorists in the early 1980s).
Take-out and restaurant.
Inexpensive - Moderate

Le Grand Colbert
2nd/Métro Bourse
2 rue Vivienne (near the Place des Victoires)
01/42.86.87.88
fax 01/42.86.82.65
Closed part of Aug.
Housed in a restored historic building, serving traditional brasserie
cuisine. Known for its seafood tray.
Moderate

A Griffonnier is a hunting dog.

Le Griffonnier
8th/Métro Champs-Elysées
8 rue des Saussaies
01/42.65.17.17
Closed Sat. & Sun.
Near the Elysée Palace, this very friendly
bistro serves reasonably priced food and wine. A great place for
lunch even if you're just looking for a salad. Don't be fooled by the
"no-smoking" section upstairs; they smoke there anyway.
Inexpensive - Moderate

Le Hangar
3rd/Métro Rambuteau
12 impasse Berthaud (off of rue Beaubourg)
01/42.74.55.44
Closed dates vary. No credit cards
Nothing fancy about this bistro near the Pompidou Center. Good
food at reasonable prices. Excellent chocolate cake.
Inexpensive

Je Thé...Me
15th/Métro Vaugirard
4 rue d'Alleray
01/48.42.48.30
Closed Sun., Mon. & Aug.

The name is a play on Je t'aime... I Love you.

This attractive bistro is in a century-old grocery store and serves
classic French fare.
Moderate

Juvenile's
1st/Métro Bourse
47 rue de Richelieu
01/42.97.46.49
fax 01/42.60.31.52
Closed Sun.
Around the corner from Willi's Wine Bar, this inexpensive, unpretentious restaurant serves light meals and has a large wine selection. Friendly and fun.
Inexpensive - Moderate

Ladurée
8th/Métro Madeleine
16 rue Royale
01/42.60.21.79
Pricey and elegant *salon de thé* and pastry shop. Also located at 8th/Métro George V, 75 avenue des Champs-Elysées 01/40.75.08.75.
Moderate - Expensive

Aux Lyonnais
2nd/Métro Bourse
32 rue St-Marc
01/42.96.65.04
fax 01/42.97.42.95
Closed Sun. & Mon. (lunch)
This beautiful century-old bistro has been recently renovated and serves the cuisine of Lyon. The wine of choice is Beaujolais.
Moderate

Ma Bourgogne   *Ma Bourgogne*
4th/Métro Saint-Paul   *another favorite.*
19 place des Vosges
01/42.78.44.64
fax 01/42.78.19.37
This café/restaurant in the place des Vosges (the oldest square in Paris) serves traditional Parisian cuisine and specializes in roast chicken.
Moderate

La Maison
5th/Métro St-Michel
1 rue de la Bûcherie
01/43.29.73.57 and 01/43.25.82.16
An interesting crowd is found at this Latin Quarter bistro located near the Seine. In good weather, the tables on the small square in front of the restaurant are a great place to dine.
Moderate

La Marée Verte
5th/Métro Maubert-Mutualité
9 rue de Pontoise
01/43.25.89.41
Closed Sun.
Traditional French cuisine (mostly seafood) in a modern setting off of the Boulevard Saint-Germain.
Moderate

Marée Verte ~
The green tide

Mariage-Frères
6th/Métro Odéon or Saint-Michel
13 rue des Grands Augustins
01/40.51.82.50
and
4th/Métro Saint-Paul or Hôtel de Ville
30-32 rue du Bourg Tibourg
01/42.72.28.11
and
8th/Métro Ternes
260 rue du Faubourg Saint-Honoré
01/46.22.18.54
400 types of teas served in elegant salons serving light meals (with no-smoking sections).
Inexpensive

Nicolas

Great place for a cheap lunch.

8th/Métro Madeleine
31 Place de la Madeleine
01/44.51.90.22
Closed Sun.
Located upstairs from the Nicolas wine shop on the
place de la Madeleine. You can buy a bottle of wine at
the shop and have it served with your meal. The menu is
limited, but the wines sold by the glass are inexpensive.
Moderate

Nos Ancêtres les Gaulois
4th/Métro Pont-Marie,
39 rue Saint-Louis-en l'Ile
01/46.33.66.07.
Sit with other tourists. The waiters are humorously rude. Loads of fun.
The food is not great, the menu is very limited, but we had a fabulous
time...though it's definitely not for everyone. It's more of an experience than a dining experience. Get reservations; it's always crowded.
Moderate

Paul-Bert
11th/Métro Faidherbe-Chaligny
18 rue Paul Bert
01/43.72.24.01
Closed Sun. & Mon.
A truly neighborhood bistro experience from its traditional decor to
its menu written on a blackboard.
Inexpensive

Pause Café
11th/Métro Ledru-Rollin
41 rue de Charonne
01/48.06.80.33
Popular café specializing in *tourtes*.
Inexpensive

Perraudin ✔

5th/Métro Luxembourg or Cluny-La Sorbonne
157 rue Saint-Jacques
No reservations
No credit cards
Closed Sat., Sun. & Mon. (lunch)
01/46.33.15.75
You'll get to know your fellow diners at this inexpensive bistro serving traditional Parisian cuisine.
Inexpensive

Le Petit Marguery

13th/Métro Gobelins
9 boulevard de Port-Royal
01/43.31.58.59
Closed Sun., Mon. & Aug.
Owned by brothers, this 1930's bistro features game dishes and is known for its good service.
Moderate

Au Petit Riche

9th/Métro Le Peletier
25 rue Le Peletier (at rue Rossini)
01/47.70.68.68
fax 01/48.24.10.79
Closed Sun.
This bistro serves specialties of the Loire Valley with a Parisian twist. Try the *civet* (game stew).
Moderate

Polidor ✔

6th/Métro Odéon
41 rue Monsieur-le-Prince
01/43.26.95.34
No reservations
No credit cards
Popular 1930's bistro serving inexpensive traditional Parisian cuisine.
Inexpensive

Le Procope
6th/Métro Odéon
13 rue de l'Ancienne Comédie
01/40.46.79.00
fax 01/40.46.79.09
Open every day to midnight
Oldest brasserie in Paris located in the Saint-Germain des Prés area.
Benjamin Franklin is said to have frequented this café. Parisian cuisine at affordable prices served in small dining rooms. Take a stroll
down the little alley behind Le Procope. It's very charming.
Moderate

Le Reminet
5th/Métro Maubert -Mutualité
5 rue des Grands Degrés
01/44.07.04.24
Closed Mon. & Tues.
Small Latin Quarter bistro with modern French cooking and attentive
service. Outdoor seating in the summer.
Moderate

Restaurant du Musée d'Orsay
7th/Métro Solférino
1 rue Légion d'Honneur
01/45.49.47.03
Open for·lunch

This restaurant is located in the beautiful Musée d'Orsay (a former
rail station) and serves a reasonably priced buffet lunch in an ornate
dining room. Not bad for a museum restaurant.
Moderate

Roger La Grenouille
6th/Métro Odéon
26 rue des Grands Augustins
01/56.24.24.34
fax 01/56.24.24.44

This quirky restaurant (it seems that everyone is having fun and the service is friendly) was founded in 1930 and serves good food at moderate prices. Especially good are the *coq au vin* and the *tournedos Rossini*.
Moderate

La Rôtisserie d'en Face
6th/Métro Odéon or St-Michel
2 rue Christine
01/43.26.40.98
fax 01/43.54.22.71

Closed Sat. (lunch) and Sun.
Modern rotisserie in the St-Germain area known for its imaginative dishes. Lots of grilled dishes on the menu.
Moderate

7ème Sud Grenelle
7th/Métro La Tour-Maubourg
159 rue de Grenelle
01/44.18.30.30
The odd name means that this restaurant is in the 7th arrondissement at the south end of rue Grenelle. This small modern restaurant serves French, Mediterranean (lots of pasta dishes) and North African (try the *tangine*) cuisine. Friendly service.
Moderate

Le Soufflé
1st/Métro Tuileries
36 rue du Mont-Thabor (between places Vendôme and Concorde)
01/42.60.27.19
fax 01/42.60.54.98
Closed Sun.
The name is deceiving, as this restaurant, known for its *soufflés*, has a full menu. It has become quite touristy, but diners praise the service.
Moderate

La Souk
11th/Métro Bastille
1 rue Keller
01/49.29.05.08
Closed Mon.
This attractive, popular Moroccan restaurant is always busy and the interior is exotic. It has a good selection of vegetarian dishes.
Moderate

La Timbre
6th/Métro Notre-Dame-des-Champs
3 rue St-Beuve
Closed Sat. (lunch) & Sun.
01/45.49.10.40
The name means "stamp" which is appropriate for this tiny Left Bank bistro. A wonderful Parisian experience. How does the English chef turn out such wonderful dishes in such a small kitchen?
Inexpensive - Moderate

Le Tire-Bouchon
15th/Métro Charles-Michels
62 rue des Entrepreneurs
01/40.59.09.27
Closed Sun., Mon. (lunch) & Sat. (lunch)
Named after the corkscrew, this small restaurant serves good food at reasonable prices.
Moderate

Le Train Bleu
12th/Métro Gare-de-Lyon
In the Gare de Lyon train station.
20 boulevard Diderot
01/43.43.09.06
fax 01/43.43.97.96
Forget all the food you've eaten in train stations. It's delicious here. But you don't really come here for the food anyway because the setting, with its murals of the French-speaking world, is spectacular. A great place to have a drink.
Expensive

Vin Sur Vin
7th/Métro Alma Marceau
20 rue de Monttessuy
01/47.05.14.20
Closed Sat. (lunch), Sun. & Mon (lunch)
Great wine and creative cuisine near the Eiffel Tower.
Moderate - Expensive

Willi's Wine Bar
1st/Métro Bourse
13 rue des Petits-Champs
01/42.61.05.09
fax 01/47.03.36.93
Closed Sun.

British owners serving Parisian specialties. A great wine list and a
favorite of many travelers to Paris.
Moderate

Yvan
8th/Métro Franklin-D.-Roosevelt
1 bis rue Jean Mermoz
01/43.59.18.40
fax 01/43.59.18.40
Closed Sat. (lunch) & Sun.
French regional and Belgian dishes in a romantic setting.
Expensive. **Le Petit Ivan** (next door) offers lower-priced dishes.

PLACES TO DRINK

Wine bars are listed above in the *Places to Eat* section of this guide.

Buddha Bar
8th/Métro Concorde
8 rue Boissy d'Anglas
01/53.05.90.00
fax 01/53.05.90.09
Asian-themed, trendy bar.

Trocadéro Dokhan's Hôtel
16th/Métro Trocadéro
117 rue Lauriston
01/53.65.66.99
fax 01/53.65.66.88
Open daily (evenings only)
An elegant champagne bar where you
can enjoy it by the flute or by the bottle.

FOOD AND WINE SHOPS

Chocolate shops (Chocolateries) and Pastry shops (Pâtisseries)

Christian Constant
6th/Métro Saint-Placide
37 rue d'Assas
01/53.63.15.15
Chocolates made with ingredients from around the world.

Lenôtre
8th/Métro Champs-Elysées – Clemenceau
10 avenue des Champs-Elysées
01/42.65.85.10
Café, kitchen shop (everything from pots and pans to wine) and
cooking school all in the elegant glass and stone Pavillon Elysée.
Lenôtre has eight other pastry shops in Paris.

La Maison du Chocolat
8th/Métro Ternes
225 rue du Faubourg-St-Honoré
01/42.27.39.44
Closed Sun.
Every chocolate lover should visit. There are also shops at 52 rue
François 1er (8th/Métro Franklin-D.-Roosevelt), 8 boulevard de la
Madeleine (9th/Métro Madeleine), 19 rue de Sèvres (6th/Métro
Sèvres Babylone), and 89 avenue Ramond Poincaré (16th/Métro
Dauphine).

Marquise de Sévigné
8th/Métro Madeleine
32 place de la Madeleine
01/42.65.19.47
A French "luxury" (their word)
chocolate maker since 1898.

The marquise de Sévigné lived in what is now the Carnavalet Museum.

A la Petite Fabrique
11th/Métro Bastille or Bréguet Sabin
12 rue Saint-Sabin
01/48.05.82.02
Closed Sun. & Mon.

Another favorite.

Our favorite chocolate store in Paris. This small and unpretentious
chocolate shop near the place de la Bastille has excellent chocolates
that make great gifts and are easy to pack to take home.

Stohrer
2nd/Métro Les Halles
51 rue Montorgueil
01/42.33.38.20
Closed part of Aug.
The Parisian favorite of *baba au rhum* was invented at this *pâtisserie*.

Candy store (Confiserie)

A La Mère de Famille
9th/Métro Le Peletier or Cadet
35 rue du Faubourg-Montmartre
01/47.70.83.69
Closed Sun., Mon. & Aug.
The oldest *confiserie* in Paris (since 1761).

A L'Etoile d'Or
9th/Métro Pigalle
30 rue Fontaine
01/48.74.59.55
Closed Mon. (morning) & Sun.
This incredible store, near the tacky sex shops of the Pigalle area,
has some of the best candy concoctions you could ever imagine.

Alléosse
17th/Métro Ternes
13 rue Poncelet
01/42.96.08.66
Closed Mon.
Shop serving rare cheeses from throughout France.

Androuët sur le Pouce
17th/Métro Villiers
23 rue du Villiers
01/47.64.39.20
Large cheese shop. This organization also operates a *bar à fromage* (cheese bar) at 49 rue St-Roch (1st/Métro Pyramides).

Barthélemy
7th/Métro Rue du Bac
51 rue de Grenelle
01/45.48.56.75
Closed Sun. & Mon.
Small cheese shop. This is where Parisians shop for their cheese.

Specialty food stores (Épiceries)

Albert Ménès
8th/Métro Madeleine or St-Augustin
41 boulevard Malesherbes
01/42.66.95.63
Closed Sun. & mid-July to mid-Aug.
Gourmet food shop that specializes in food from the provinces.

Boutique Maille
8th/Métro Madeleine
6 place de la Madeleine
01/40.15.06.00
Closed Sun.
Boutique mustard shop on the
place de la Madeleine.

Caviar Kaspia
8th/Métro Madeleine
17 place de la Madeleine
01/42.65.33.32 (restaurant)/01/42.65.66.21 (store)
Closed Sun.
Caviar, blinis and salmon. There's also a restaurant upstairs.

Fauchon
8th/Métro Madeleine
26 place de la Madeleine
01/47.42.60.11
Closed Sun.

Do not touch the food! A clerk must get it for you.

Deli and grocery known for its huge selection of canned food, baked goods and alcohol. The store is a must for those wanting to bring back French specialties. Fauchon also has carry-out food, wine and pastry shops at 14 locations throughout Paris. They open early, close late. Locations include 10 rue Saint-Antoine (4th/Métro Bastille).

Gourmet Lafayette
8th/Métro Chaussée-d'Antin
40 boulevard Hausmann (in the Galeries Lafayette department store)
01/42.82.34.56
Closed Sun.
This department store has a huge gourmet-food section.

La Grande Épicerie
7th/Métro Sèvres Babylone
38 rue Sèvres (in the Au Bon Marché department store)
01/44.39.81.00
Closed Sun.
The ultimate grocery store (with wine cellar and carry-out).

Hédiard
8th/Métro Madeleine
21 place de la Madeleine
01/43.12.88.88
Closed Sun.
Food store/spice shop that has been open since the 1850's, similar to Fauchon, with an on-site restaurant (01/43.12.88.99).

La Maison du Miel
9th/Métro Opéra or Madeleine
24 rue Vignon
01/47.42.26.70
Closed Sun.
This food store contains everything made from honey (from sweets to soap) and is located around the corner from Fauchon.

Oliviers & Co.
Olive oils from around the Mediterranean at several lovely shops:
2nd/90 rue Montorgueil, 4th/47 rue
Vieille du Temple, 4th/81 rue St Louis en
l'Ile, 5th/128 rue Mouffetard. 6th/28 rue
de Buci, 7th/44 rue Cler, 15th/85 rue du
Commerce, and 17th/8 bis rue de Lévis

Great for Souveniers.

Wine stores (Caves)

L'Amour du Vin
7th/Métro Ecole-Militaire
94 rue Saint-Dominique
01/45.56.12.94
A large selection of reasonably priced wines.

The Love of Wine.

Les Caves Augé
8th/Métro Saint-Augustin
116 boulevard Haussmann
01/45.22.16.97
Famous wine shop since 1850.

Lavinia
1st/Métro Madeleine
3-5 boulevard de la Madeleine
01/42.97.20.20
Closed Sun. Open until 8:00 p.m.
The largest wine shop in Paris with 2000 foreign wines, 3000 French wines and 1000 spirits, priced from 3 to 3600 euros. Drink any bottle from the shop at the wine bar.
Lunch served with wine, of course. No dinner.

Caves Estève

4th/Métro Bastille
10 rue de la Cerisaie
01/42.72.33.05
Reasonably priced wines at this popular wine shop. Locations also in the 5th/Métro Port-Royal, 292 rue Saint-Jacques, and in the 4th/Métro Bastille, 7 rue de la Cerisale.

Les Caves Taillevent

8th/Métro Charles-de-Gaulle-Étoile or Saint-Philippe-du-Roule
199 rue du Faubourg-Saint-Honoré
01/45.61.14.09
This wine shop is associated with the well-known Taillevent restaurant and is said to have over 500,000 bottles of wine starting at around $5. You'll be amazed at the cost of some selections.

La Dernière Goutte

The last drop.

6th/Métro Mabillon
6 rue de Bourbon-le-Château
01/43.29.11.62
Located in an old vaulted room. The owners are charming and friendly and they generally have wine tastings.

Nicolas

Over 250 wine stores located throughout Paris.
The main one is in the 8th/Métro Madeleine at
31 Place de la Madeleine.
01/44.51.90.22
www.nicolas-wines.com
Closed Sun.

If you're looking for a comprehensive guide to speaking French, this is not the right place. What follows are simply a few tips for speaking French and a very brief pronunciation guide.

It is always good to learn a few polite terms so that you can excuse yourself when you've stepped on the foot of an elderly lady or spilled your drink down the back of the gentleman in front of you. It's also just common courtesy to greet the people you meet in your hotel, in shops and restaurants in their own language.

If a word ends in a consonant and that word is followed by a word that starts in a vowel, the consonant is linked to the vowel. So, **vous avez** (you have) is pronounced voozavay. And the final consonant in a word is silent (unless followed by an e).

a like in far
e like in open
é and ez like the a in rate
è like the e in bet
ê like eh as in *crêpe*
i like the i in machine
o like the o in not
ô like the o in wrote
u round your lips as to say oh, but say ee
an, am, en, em, ant, ent like the a in wand
au, eau like the o in okay
er at the end of a word sounds like the ay in day
in, im, ain, aim like the a in sank
ou like the oo in cool
oi like the wa in water
que like the cu in curve
qui like kee

un is pronounced uhn
c like a k before a, o, u and consonants
c like an s before e and i
ch like sh
ç like the s in simple
g before a, o and u like in good
g like the s in pleasure before i and e
gn like the ny in canyon
h is always silent
j like the s in measure
r like an r being swallowed
s like the s in step but when between vowels, it's pronounced like a z
ss like an s
zh like the s in measure

46

*This is a brief listing of some
familiar English foods and
food-related words that you
may need in a restaurant setting. It is followed by a list of
phrases that may come in
handy. There are also some
pronunciation prompts. They
aren't all exactly right, but
they're close enough to get you
what you need.*

allergic, allergique *anchois ~*
anchovies, anchois *an-shwa*
appetizer, hors-d'oeuvre
apple, pomme
artichoke, artichaut
ashtray, cendrier
asparagus, aspèrge
bacon, lard (lardons)
baked, au four/cuit au four
banana, banane
beans, fève
beef, boeuf
beefsteak, bifteck/steak
beer, bière
beverages, boissons
bill, l'addition
bitter, amer
boiled, bouilli
bottle (half), demi-bouteille
bottle, bouteille *boutielle ~*
bowl, bol *boo-tay*
braised, braisé
bread, pain
bread roll, petit pain

breakfast, petit déjeuner
broth, consommé
butter, beurre
cabbage, chou
cake, gâteau
candle, chandelle/bougie
carrot, carotte
cereal, céréale(s)
chair, chaise
check, chèque
cheers, santé
cheese, fromage
cherry, cerise
chicken, poulet
chicken breast, suprême de
    volaille
chops, côtelettes, côtes
clams, palourdes
cocktail, cocktail
cod, morue
coffee, café
coffee (American-style), café
    américain
coffee w/milk, café crème/un
crème (*café au lait* if you want
    a lot of milk)
coffee (black), café noir
coffee (decaf), déca/décafféiné
cold, froid
corn, maïs
cover charge, couvert
credit card, carte de crédit
cucumber, concombre
cup, tasse
custard, crème anglaise
dessert, dessert
dinner, dîner

dish (plate), assiette. A main
  dish is *plat principal*
drink, boisson
duck, canard
eggs, oeufs
espresso, café express/un
  express
fish, poisson
fish soup, bouillabaisse (the
  famous seafood stew)
fork, fourchette
french fries, frites (pommes
  frites)
fresh, fraîche/frais
fried, frit
fruit, fruits
game, gibier
garlic, ail
gin, gin
glass, verre
goat, chèvre
goose, oie
grapefruit, pamplemousse
grapes, raisin
green beans, haricots verts
grilled, grillé
ham (cooked), jambon (cuit)
ham (cured), jambon (de
  Parme & de Bayonne)
hamburger, hamburger
honey, miel
hot, chaud
ice, glaçon
ice cream, glace
ice (on the rocks), avec des
  glaçons
ice water, l'eau glacée

[handwritten: ail ~ aye]
[handwritten: Chaud ~ Froid]
[handwritten: SHOW ~ FWA]

included, compris
ketchup, ketchup
knife, couteau *[handwritten: Couteau - coo.toe]*
kosher, casher/kascher
lamb, agneau
large, grand
lemon, citron
lettuce, laitue
little, petit/peu de...
liver, foie *[handwritten: déjeuner ~]*
lobster, homard *[handwritten: day-juh-nay]*
loin, longe (pork)/aloyau (beef)
lunch, déjeuner
match, allumette
mayonnaise, mayonnaise
meat, viande
medium (cooked), à point
melon, melon
menu, carte
milk, lait
  Lait écrémé is skim milk
  & *lait entier*, whole milk
mineral water, eau minérale
mineral water (sparkling),
  eau minérale (gazeuse)
**mineral water (w/out carbon-
  ation),** eau minérale plate (non
  gazeuse)
mixed, mélange, mixte,
  mesclun (salad greens)
mushrooms, champignons
mussels, moules
mustard, moutarde
napkin, serviette
noodles, pâtes/nouilles
nuts, noix
octopus, poulpes

oil, huile

olive oil, huile d'olive

olives, olives

omelette, omelette

on the rocks (w/ ice), avec des glaçons

onions, oignons *oignons ~*

orange, orange *ON-yone*

orange juice, jus d'orange

overdone, trop cuit *huitres ~*

oysters, huîtres *weeT-RAH*

partridge, perdrix

pastry, pâtisserie

peaches, pêches

pears, poires

peas, petits pois

pepper (black), poivre

peppers (sweet), poivrons

perch, perche

pineapple, ananas

plate (dish), assiette

please, s'il vous plaît

plums, prunes

poached, poché

pork, porc

potatoes, pommes de terre

poultry, volaille

prawns, grosses crevettes/ langoustines

quail, caille

rabbit, lapin

rare, saignant

raspberry, framboises

receipt, note/reçu

rice, riz

roast, rôti

rolls, petits pains

salad, salade

salmon, saumon

salt, sel

sandwich, sandwich(e)

sauce, sauce

sautéed, sauté

scallops, coquilles (Saint-Jacques) *brouille ~*

scrambled, brouillé *brew-ee*

seafood, fruits de mer

seasonings, condiments/ assaisonnement

shellfish, crustacés

shrimp, crevettes

small, petit

smoked, fumé

snails, escargots

sole, sole

soup, soupe

spaghetti, spaghetti

sparkling (wine), champagne

specialty, spécialité *epicé ~*

spicy, épicé *AY-PEE-SAY*

spinach, épinards

spoon, cuiller/cuillère

squid, calmar/calamar

steak, steak/bifteck

steamed, vapeur

stew, ragoût

strawberries, fraises

sugar, sucre

sugar substitute, édulcorant/de l'aspartam

supper, dîner

sweet, doux/sucré

table, table

tea, thé

tea w/lemon, thé citron
tea w/milk, thé au lait
thank you, merci
tip, pourboire
toast, pain grillé *grillé ~ gree-AY*
tomato, tomate
toothpick, cure-dents
trout, truite
tuna, thon
turkey, dindon/dinde
utensil, couvert
veal, veau
vegetable, légume
vegetarian, végétarien
venison, venaison
vinegar, vinaigre
vodka, vodka
waiter, monsieur (never *garçon*)
waitress, madame or mademoiselle
water, eau
watermelon, pastèque
well done, bien cuit. Very well done is *très bien cuit*
whipped cream, crème chantilly *(shan-tee-ee)*
wine, vin
wine list, carte des vins
wine (red), vin rouge
wine (rosé), vin rosé
wine (white), vin blanc
with, avec
without, sans
yogurt, yaourt

Helpful phrases
please, s'il vous plaît
thank you, merci
yes, oui
no, non
good morning, bonjour
good afternoon, bonjour
good evening, bonsoir
good night, bonne nuit
goodbye, au revoir

Do you speak English?, parlez-vous anglais?
I don't speak French, je ne parle pas français
excuse me, pardon
I don't understand, je ne comprends pas
I'd like a table, je voudrais une table
I'd like to reserve a table, je voudrais réserver une table
for one person, pour une personne *-UNE*
for two, pour deux *- deh*
--trois (3) *-Twa*
--quatre (4) *- CaT*
--cinq (5) *- Sank*
--six (6) *- See*
--sept (7) *- SeT*
--huit (8) *- weeT*
--neuf (9) *- nurf*
--dix (10) *- deece*

this evening, ce soir

tomorrow, demain

near the window, près de la fenêtre

with a view, avec vue

outside on the patio, sur la terrasse

no smoking, non-fumeur (don't count on this in France)

where is?, où est

where are?, où sont

the bathrooms, les toilettes

the bill, l'addition

a mistake (error), une erreur

Is service included?, Le service est-il compris?

Do you accept credit cards?, acceptez-vous les cartes de crédit

traveler's checks, chèques de voyage

How much is it?, c'est combien?

What is this?, qu'est-ce que c'est?

I did not order this, ce n'est pas ce que j'ai commandé

This is, c'est

—too, trop — *Trow*

—cold, froid — *FWA*

—hot, chaud — *SHOw*

—not fresh, n'est pas frais — *NAY PAH FRAIS*

—rare, saignant — *SANE-YANT*

—undercooked, pas assez cuit — *PAH AHSAY CWEE*

—overcooked, trop cuit *TROW CWEE*

—delicious, délicieux

I am a vegeterian, Je suis végétarien(ne)

without meat, pas de viande/sans viande

closed, fermé

Monday, lundi	*Lundee*	
Tuesday, mardi	*Mardee*	
Wednesday, mercredi	*Mare KRAdee*	
Thursday, jeudi	*Juhdee*	
Friday, vendredi	*Vawndradee*	
Saturday, samedi	*Sumahdee*	
Sunday, dimanche	*Dee mansh*	

MENU READER

AAAAA, the seal of approval of
*l'Association Amicale des Amateurs
d'Andouillettes Authentiques.*
Only in France would they have an
association for devotees of
andouillette (tripe sausage)

In French Amateur means "Lover of "

abats, abattis, organ meats

abricot, apricot

acras/accras, *beignets,* usually stuffed
w/seafood, found in the French West Indies

acidulé, acidic

addition (l'addition), check/bill

affinée, aged

agneau, lamb

agneau de lait, milk-fed lamb

agneau pré-salé, lamb grazed on salt marshes

agrumes, citrus fruits

Agrumes.

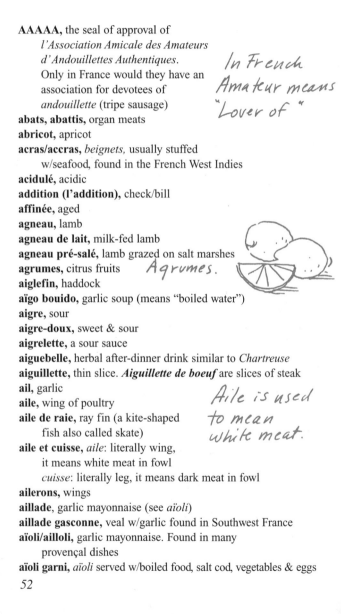

aiglefin, haddock

aïgo bouido, garlic soup (means "boiled water")

aigre, sour

aigre-doux, sweet & sour

aigrelette, a sour sauce

aiguebelle, herbal after-dinner drink similar to *Chartreuse*

aiguillette, thin slice. *Aiguillette de boeuf* are slices of steak

ail, garlic

aile, wing of poultry

Aile is used to mean white meat.

aile de raie, ray fin (a kite-shaped
fish also called skate)

aile et cuisse, *aile:* literally wing,
it means white meat in fowl
cuisse: literally leg, it means dark meat in fowl

ailerons, wings

aillade, garlic mayonnaise (see *aïoli*)

aillade gasconne, veal w/garlic found in Southwest France

aïoli/ailloli, garlic mayonnaise. Found in many
provençal dishes

aïoli garni, *aïoli* served w/boiled food, salt cod, vegetables & eggs

airelle, cranberry

à la, à l', au, aux, in the manner of, in, with

à la carte, side dishes (each item ordered separately)

albert, a sauce of egg yolk, cream, horseradish, shallots & mustard

albuféra, *béchamel* sauce w/sweet peppers

alcool, alcohol

algues, seaweed

ali baba, spongecake soaked in rum

aligot, garlic mashed potatoes w/cheese

alimentation, food/food store

allumettes, puff pastry or potato strips

alose, shad (fish)

alouette, lark

alouette sans tête, rolled veal slice
    stuffed w/garlic & minced meat

Alouettes Sans têtes~ Larks without heads!

aloyau, sirloin

Alsace, located in the northeast corner of France (along the
    German border); one of France's wine regions specializing
    in white wines such as Gewürztraminer, Riesling, Pinot Gris,
    Pinot Blanc, Pinot Noir & Sylvaner

alsacienne, alsacien/usually garnished w/sausage & sauerkraut
    (means "Alsace style")

amande, almond

amande de mer, small shellfish

amandine, w/almonds

amer/amère, bitter

américaine, white wine sauce usually w/brandy,
    shallots, tomatoes & garlic w/shrimp/lobster

Amer Picon, aperitif (wine & brandy w/herbs)

amidon, starch. *Amidon de blé* is cornstarch

amourettes, the bone marrow of an ox or calf

amuse-bouche, appetizer

amuse-gueule, appetizer

ananas, pineapple

anchoïade, anchovy spread from Provence

anchois, anchovy

ancienne, "old style": usually means a
    wine cream sauce w/mushrooms,
    shallots or onions

andalouse, usually w/eggplant, tomatoes
    & green peppers

Bouche ~ mouth guevle ~ throat These are small morsels of food Just a mouthful or two.

andouille, tripe sausage
andouillette, small tripe sausage
aneth, dill
angélique, the crystallized stalks of
the herb angelica
(a decoration for cakes)
anglaise, boiled/boiled or steamed
vegetables/breaded, fried meat,
fish or vegetables
anguille, eel. Many dishes in the French West Indies feature eels
anguille au vert, eel in a white sauce w/parsley
anis, aniseed
apéritif, drink before dinner
à point, medium rare
appellation d`origine contrôlée, an officially recognized wine
of France. Sometimes designated by A.O.C. The makers of
A.O.C. are the best of the French wine industry
arachide, peanut
araignée de mer, spider crab
ardennaise, usually means served w/berries ("Ardennes style")
ardoise, specials are often written on the *ardoise*, a chalk board.
This can also mean (for regular customers) that they put it
on your running bill
arête, fish bone
argenteuil, asparagus soup
arlequin, two flavors
armagnac, brandy (similar to *cognac*). The main difference is
cognac is distilled twice (& thus smoother)
while *armagnac* is distilled only once
armoricaine, in a tomato sauce
arôme, aroma
aromates, herbs & spices
aromatisé, flavored
artichaut, artichoke
artichauts à la barigoule, artichokes w/mushrooms & pork
artichaut violet, small artichoke
asperge, asparagus
asperge à la flamande, white asparagus w/egg sauce.
A Belgian specialty
asperge d'Argenteuil, large white artichoke
aspic, gelatin

We have a general rule about tripe: Don't. But we love andouillette.

aspic de volaille, chicken in aspic

assaisonnement, dressing/seasoning

assiette, plate

assiette anglaise, cold cuts

assiette de charcuterie, assorted meat products (cold cuts)

assiette de crudités, a plate of raw vegetables

assiette du pêcheur, assorted fish plate

assorti, assorted

asturienne, w/livers

au, in

aubergine, eggplant

aulx, garlic (the plural of *ail*)

Aubergine.

aumônière, *crêpe* filled & wrapped into the shape of a little
   purse. The word means "beggar's purse"

aurore, a tomato sauce

auvergnat, usually means served w/sausage & cabbage (means
   "Auvergne style")

aux, with

avec, with

avec des glaçons, on the rocks

avocat, avocado

avoine, oats

aziminu, Corsican *bouillabaisse*

Avec des glaçons.

baba au rhum, spongecake soaked in rum

bäckaoffa, meat & potato stew from Alsace

bacon, Canadian bacon

baeckeoffe, baked meat &
   potato stew from Alsace

bagna cauda, hot anchovy dip from Provence

baguette, long & thin loaf of bread

baies, berries

baigné, bathed

ballottine (de volaille), boned meat
   (poultry) stuffed, rolled,
   cooked & served in gelatin

*Ballotine.
Not sure
about this
concept.*

banane, banana

bananes flambées, bananas flamed in brandy

bananes vertes, green bananas used in dishes in the
   French West Indies

Bandol, popular wine from Provence. The red is full-bodied
   & spicy & the white is fruity, often with a hint of aniseed

banon, cheese from Provence dipped in *eau-de-vie* & wrapped in chestnut leaves

bar, bass

barbarie, Barbary (a type of duck)

barbouiado, vegetable *ragoût*

barbue, brill (fish)

barde, the lard or bacon put over roasts

barigoule, artichoke hearts, sausage, bacon, garlic & mushroom dish

Barigoule. Like the sound of it

baron, the hindquarter & leg of a lamb

barquette, small boat-shaped pastry. *Une barquette* means "a carton of"

Barry, à la du, served w/a cauliflower & cheese sauce

basilic, basil

basquaise, served w/tomatoes, or red peppers ("Basque style")

bâtard, a small *baguette*

batonnets, crisp sticks. *Batonnets de courgette* are crisp zucchini sticks

baudroie, monkfish
This can also refer to a fish soup w/garlic & vegetables

bavaroise, custard dessert

bavette, flank steak

béarnaise, *hollandaise* sauce w/vinegar, tarragon, shallots & wine

Sauce Bearnaise.

béatilles, mixed organ meats

beaufort, a hard cheese

Beaujolais, one of France's wine regions (on the south tip of Burgundy) noted for fruity red wines. *Beaujolais Nouveau* is light & fruity & denotes the first wine to be released

beaumont, a mild cheese

bécasse, woodcock

bécassine, snipe

béchamel, white sauce (usually butter, milk [&/or cream] & flour)

beckenoff, pork & mutton baked w/potatoes

beignet, fritter filled w/fruit, meat &/or vegetables (a filled doughnut)

belle étoile, a mild cheese

belon, a type of oyster

bénédictine, dark green, brandy-based liqueur

Belle étoile ~ beautiful star.

bergamotte, a variety of lemon or pear

bercy, fish stock *velouté* w/white wine,
    shallots & parsley

berlingots, mint-flavored caramels

betterave, beet

beuchelle, creamed kidneys &
    sweetbreads

Bettrave.

beurgoule, caramel-rice pudding

beurre, butter

beurre blanc, white butter sauce of
    white wine, vinegar & shallots

beurre blanc nantais, white butter & shallot sauce for fish

beurre d'ail, garlic butter

beurre d'anchois, anchovy butter

beurre de montpellier, green butter (made green from herbs)

beurre d'estragon, tarragon butter

beurre fondu, melted butter

beurre maître d'hôtel, butter w/chopped parsley & lemon juice

beurre manié, butter & flour thickening for sauces

beurre nantais, white butter

beurre noir, browned butter sauce
    (until it's almost black)

beurre noisette, lightly browned butter

bicard de soude, baking soda

biche, female deer

bien cuit, well done

bière, beer

bière à la pression, draft beer

bière blonde, lager beer

Bière.

bière brune, dark beer

bière légère, light beer

bifteck, beef steak

biftek de cheval, horse-meat steak

bigarade, brown sauce usually w/vinegar, sugar & oranges

bigarreau, a type of cherry

bigorneaux, small sea mollusks

bigourneau, the shellfish periwinkle

billes de melons, melon balls

billy bi, cream of mushroom soup

biscotte, zwieback (sweetened bread enriched w/eggs, baked &
    sliced & toasted until dry & crisp)

biscuit, biscuit/cookie
biscuit à la cuillère, ladyfingers
biscuit de Savoie, spongecake
biscuits aux brisures de chocolat,
    chocolate-chip cookies
bisque, chowder
bisque d'écrevisses, freshwater
    crayfish chowder
bisque de homard, lobster bisque
bisque de langoustines, saltwater
    crayfish chowder
blaff, spicy stewed fresh fish
    dish served in the
    French West Indies
blanc, white
blanc-cassis, white wine &
    black currant liqueur

*Bisque de...
ecrevisses, homard,
Langoustines...
Love 'em all.*

blanc de blancs, white wine made from white grapes
blanc de poireau, the white part of a leek
blanc de volaille, boned breast of poultry
blanchaille, whitebait, a fish
blanchi, blanched
blanquette, stew
blanquette de veau, veal
    stew in a white sauce
blé, wheat
blé de turquie, corn
blé dur, duram wheat
blette, Swiss chard

*Blanc Cassis
is a popular
aperatif
in France.*

bleu, blue cheese/meat prepared nearly raw/fish boiled very
    fresh. Some popular blue cheeses
    are bleu d'Auvergne, bleu de Bresse,
    bleu des Causses & bleu du Haut-Jura
blini, small pancakes (usually w/sour
    cream, caviar & salmon)
blonde, light (as in light-colored
    [lager] beer)
boeuf, beef

*In Canada
Blonde means
girl friend
no matter what
color her hair is.*

boeuf à la ficelle, beef cooked in stock
boeuf à la gardiane, beef & wine stew w/black olives
boeuf à la gordienne, braised beef dish from Provence

boeuf à la mode, beef marinated in red wine

boeuf bourguignon, beef stewed in red wine (burgundy) w/onions, bacon & mushrooms

boeuf braisé à la beauceronne, beef casserole found around Orléans

boeuf en daube, larded chunks of beef marinated & cooked in wine/beef casserole

boeuf miroton, beef stew or boiled beef w/onion sauce

boeuf mode, beef stew w/carrots. This can also refer to cold beef in jelly

boeuf salé, corned beef

bohémienne, eggplant & tomato casserole. A specialty in Nice

boisson, beverage

boissons compris, drinks included

boissons non compris, drinks not included

boîte, can, box or jar. *Une boîte de conserve...* means a can of...

boles de picolat, meatballs & mushrooms cooked in a sauce

bolet, boletus mushroom

bombe/bombe glacée, layered ice cream

bon, bonne, good

bonbons, candy

bonne femme, homestyle cooking. This can also refer to a *sauce veloutée* w/*crème fraîche* & lemon juice

Bonne femme means Good Woman.

bonnefoy, *sauce velouté* w/shallots & white wine

Bordeaux, one of France's wine regions (the largest wine-producing area in the world). Red *Bordeaux* is made from a blend of cabernet sauvignon, merlot, cabernet franc, malbec & petite verdot grapes. White *Bordeaux* is made from semillon & sauvignon blanc grapes.

bordelaise, red wine sauce w/mushrooms, beef marrow & shallots

botte, bunch (as in a bunch of herbs). *Botte de radis* means bunch of radishes

bouchée, bite size. *Cidre bouché* refers to alcoholic, dry cider

bouchée à la reine, puff pastry filled w/meat, seafood, sweet breads &/or mushrooms

boucherie, butcher shop. *Boucheries chevalines* are still found in France & are horse-meat butcher shops

bouchon, cork

boudin, blood sausage (black pudding)

boudin blanc, white sausage
(sausage of white meats)
boudin liège, Belgian sausage
boudin noir (boudin antillais), spicy
blood sausage (a specialty
in the French West Indies)
bougon, a goat's milk cheese
bouillabaisse, shellfish & fish stewed
in white wine, olive oil, saffron,
tomatoes & garlic. There are many versions of this dish
bouilli, boiled/boiled beef
bouillon, broth/stock
boulanger, baker. *Boulangère* is a woman baker
boulangerie, bakery
boule de fromage frit, fried cheese ball
boulette, meatball or fishball
boulette de semoule, semolina & potato *gnocchi*
boulghour, bulgur wheat
boullinade, thick soup found in the South of France
bouquet, large (red) shrimp (usually served cold)
bouquet garni, a small bundle of herbs
&/or spices tied together in
cheesecloth & used to provide
flavor to dishes while they cook
bouquet rose, prawns
bourbon, bourbon
bourboulhade, salt cod & garlic soup.
Sometimes referred to as
a poor man's *bouillabaisse*
bourdaines, apples baked in pastry
bourdaloue, butter cake w/fruit
Bourgogne, Burgundy. Burgundy is one of France's wine
regions (famous for red wines made from pinot noir grapes)
Bourgueil, light, fruity wine from the Loire Valley
bourguignon/bourguignonne, mushrooms & onions in a red
wine sauce (see *boeuf bourguignon*)
bouribut, red wine duck stew
bourride, a fish stew found in the South of France (thickened
w/egg yolks & *aïoli*)
boursin, a mild, soft cheese
boutargue, smoked fish roe

Boudin is also an unflattering term for a woman.

Bouquet garni can be found in boxes packaged like tea bags and are great.

bouteille, bottle

braisé, braised

braiser, to braise

branches de céleri, celery stalks

brandade, cod & potato dish

brandade de morue, salt cod w/garlic, cream & olive oil

brandy, brandy

brebis, sheep's-milk cheese

brème, bream

Bretagne, Brittany, an Atlantic coastal province

bretonne, usually a dish served w/white wine sauce or white beans ("Brittany style"). This can also refer to a type of oyster

brézzolles, slices of veal

bricks, round, paper-thin sheets of pastry (usually filled w/egg & Middle Eastern spices). A specialty of Tunisia

brie, white, mellow, soft cheese. If you don't know what *brie* is, you shouldn't be in France

brins, branches or sprigs

brioche, small sweet cake or roll

broccio, a cheese (similar to *ricotta*) found in Corsica

broche, (on a) spit

brochet, pike

brochette de coeurs, heart kabob. A specialty in Toulouse

brochette, en, cooked on a skewer

brocoli, broccoli

broufado, braised beef w/anchovies

brouillade d'aubergines, stuffed eggplant w/tomatoes

brouillé, scrambled

Brouilly, red wine from Beaujolais

brousse de brebis, soft & mild sheep's- or goat's-milk cheese

brousse du Rove, cheese (similar to *ricotta*) made w/sheep's milk. The sheep graze on thyme, which gives the cheese its unusual flavor

brugnon, nectarine

brûlé, burned/caramelized

brune, dark (as in dark beer)

brunoise, diced vegetables

brut, very dry

Bouteille ~ Boo t ay

Brins de romarin.

Brugnon.

bûche de Noël, rolled Christmas cake

Bûche de Noël.

buffet froid, a variety of cold dishes
bugnes, fried doughnuts
buisson, vegetable dish
bulot, large sea snail
Burgundy, a wine (red, white or rosé) produced in the
    Burgundy region
Byrrh, sweet wine (fortified w/brandy) mixed w/quinine
cabécou, a strong, round goat cheese
Cabernet Sauvignon, dry red wine
cabillaud, cod
cabri, kid goat
cacahuète, peanut

Cafe Americain.

cacao, cocoa
cachat, fresh cheese from Provence
Caen, à la mode de, cooked w/*calvados*
café, coffee (really, espresso)
café américain, American-style coffee
café au lait, coffee w/milk
café brûlot, flaming coffee
    (strong coffee w/liquor
    which is set on fire)
café complet, continental breakfast
    (coffee, bread, butter & jam)
café crème, coffee w/cream
café déca, decaffeinated coffee
café décaféiné, decaffeinated coffee
café de Paris, the name for a butter
    sauce flavored w/cognac & herbs
café espresso, espresso
café express, espresso
café filtre, drip-brewed coffee/
    American-style coffee
café frappé, iced coffee
café glacé, coffee-flavored ice
    cream/iced coffee
café liégeois, cold coffee
    served w/ice cream
café nature, black coffee
café noir, black coffee
café sans caféine, decaffeinated coffee

If you want to order American coffee without seeming so... American, you can order Café élongée. (AY-Lon-jay) It's just French coffee "elongated" with water.

café soluble, instant coffee
café viennois, coffee w/whipped cream
cagouille, small land snail
caille, quail
caillete, pâté of pork, herbs & garlic
calalou, "pepperpot" stew w/many
    ingredients found in the French West Indies
calamar, squid
calissons, marzipan candies
    shaped like boats from Aix
calmar, squid
calvados, apple brandy
camembert, soft cheese w/strong flavor
camomille, camomile tea
campagne, à la, this term means "country style" & has many
    different meanings
canapé, appetizer w/bread base & topped w/various ingredients
canard, duck
canard à la presse, roast duck dish w/red wine & Cognac
canard à l'orange, roast duck braised w/orange sauce
canard de Barbarie, a duck breed in Southwest France
canard de Challans, a type of small duck
canard de Nantes, a type of small duck
canard de Rouen, a type of wild duck
canard laqué, Peking duck
canard Montmorency, duck w/cherries
canard rôti, roast duck
canard sauvage, wild duck
cancoillotte, strong, hard cheese (melted before serving) from
    the Franche-Comté region in Eastern France
candi, candied
caneton, duckling
canette, young female duck
canistrelli, dry cookies from Corsica
cannelle, cinnamon
cantal, a cheese very much like cheddar
caouanne, turtle
capoun fassum, cabbage stuffed w/rice & sausage
câpre, caper
caqhuse, pork & onion casserole
carafe, carafe

caramélisé, caramelized

caramel, burned sugar. This also refers to a chewy vanilla or chocolate caramel

carapaces, shells

carbonnade, braised beef stew (a Belgian specialty) also charcoal-grilled meat

carbonnade à la boeuf, Belgian specialty of beef marinated in beer & cooked in onions & herbs

carbonnade bruxelloise, Belgian dish of pork w/a tomato & tarragon sauce

carbonnade flamande, beef, herbs & onions braised in beer

carbonnade nîmoise, lamb & potato dish

cardinal, fish stock *velouté*, lobster, butter & cream

cardomome, cardamom

cardon, cardoon (a member of the thistle family)

cargolade, grilled snail dish from Languedoc-Roussillon

cari, curry

carotte, carrot

carottes glacées, carrots glazed in butter

carottes râpées, grated carrots

carottes Vichy, steamed carrots (in butter & parsley)

carpe, carp

carré, rack/loin/fillet

carré d'agneau, rack or loin of lamb

carré de l'Est, pungent cheese (square shaped)

carré de porc, rack or loin of pork

carré de veau, rack or loin of veal

carrelet, flounder/plaice

carte, la, menu

carte des vins, wine list

carvi, caraway seeds

casse-croûte, snack ("breaking the crust")

casse-pierre, seaweed

cassis, black currant/black currant liqueur

cassolette, dish served in a small casserole

cassoulet (toulousain), meat & bean (& often sausage) casserole. This dish originated in Southwest France

castagna, chestnut in Corsican

Carapaces refers to shrimp or Lobster Shells.

The French are not so much for snacking, Casse-croute refers to a small-meal type snack.

castanhet, chestnut cake

cavaillon, a fragrant melon from the town of the same name in Provence. It looks like a small cantaloupe

cave, wine shop/wine cellar

caviar, fish eggs

Celeri.

caviar d'aubergine, eggplant purée

cédrat, citron

céleri, celery

céleri-rave, celery root

céleri rémoulade, celery root in a creamy mayonnaise dressing

cendre chemisée, smoldering

cèpe, boletus mushroom

céréale, cereal

cerf, venison (deer)

cerfeuil, chervil

cerise, cherry

cerise noire, black cherry

Cerf.

cerises jubilé, cherries flamed w/*kirsch* & served w/ice cream

cerneau, the "meat" of a walnut

cervelas, seasoned sausage made from brains

Cervelle.
Apparently
some people
like it.

cervelle, brains

cervelle de canut, herbed cheese spread

chabichou, cow's- & goat's-milk cheese. Some think it has a sweet flavor

Chablis, one of France's wine regions producing white wine made from the chardonnay grape

chair, "fleshy" part of fish or meat

Challonaise, wine region producing mostly table wine

chambré, room temperature (when serving wine)

Champagne, A region in Northeastern France famous for its sparkling wines classified by the sugar content. ***Brut*** is the driest, ***extra-sec*** is very dry, ***sec*** is dry, ***demi-sec*** is slightly sweet & ***doux*** is sweet. Also a sweet cookie served w/champagne

champenoise, sparkling wine

champêtre, this term means "rustic" & can mean many things – usually it signifies a simple dish

champignon, mushroom

champignon à la grecque, cold mushroom appetizer

Champignons.

65

champignon de bois, wild mushroom

champignon de Paris, button mushroom

champignon de pin, pine mushroom.
 A wild mushroom found in Provence

champignon sauvage, wild mushroom

changement de garniture, this means an extra charge for
 substitutions

chansons aux pommes, flaky breakfast
 pastry w/apple filling

Chansons aux pommes means Songs to apples.

chanterelle, chanterelle mushroom

chantilly, sweet whipped cream.
 This can also refer to
 hollandaise sauce & whipped cream

chaource, cheese found in the Champagne region

chapelure, breadcrumbs

chapon, capon

chapon de mer, scorpion fish

charbonnade, charcoal-grilled meat

charcuterie, can be a deli or any
 place serving prepared meats & salads.
 This can also refer to cooked pork meats/cold cuts

charcuterie assortie, assorted cold meats

chariot, dessert &/or cheese cart

Chariot... be on the Lookout!

charlotte, fruit dessert made in a
 mold/baked fruit compote/pudding

charolais, denotes a high-quality beef

chartreuse, yellow (or green) herb liqueur. Also a game bird
 (usually pheasant or partridge) dish from Alsace

chasse, venison

chasselas, a white grape

chasseur, "hunter's style" usually means
 in a sauce w/tomatoes,
 wine, herbs & mushrooms

Chasse means hunt.

châtaigne, chestnut

châtaignes chaudes/marrons chauds, roasted chestnuts

chateaubriand, thick slice of tenderloin stuffed w/sauteed
 shallots & usually served
 w/butter or *béarnaise* sauce

Château-Margaux, red wine from Bordeaux

Châteauneuf-du-Pape, red wine from
 the Rhône River valley

Châteauneuf du Pape means the Pope's new castle.

chaud, hot

chaud-froid, cold poultry dish/a dish containing gelatin. It's cooked & then served cold, thus the name which means "hot-cold"

chaudrée, seafood & fish stew (contains the white part of squid)

chauffé, heated

chaumes, rich, creamy cheese from Dordogne

chausson, fruit turnover

chausson aux pommes, apple turnover

chemise, en, baked in parchment/wrapped in pastry/potato w/the skin left on

cheval, horse

chèvre, goat/goat cheese

chevreau, young goat

chèvre fraîche, goat cheese which is only a few days old

chèvre sèche, dried (aged) goat cheese

chevreuil, deer

chichi, orange-flavored doughnuts/can also mean "fancy"

chicons du Nord, Belgian endive

chicorée, chicory/endive

chicorée frisée, curly lettuce

chicorée witloof, Belgian endive

chiffonnade, shredded leafy vegetables & herbs

chinchard, saurel, a fish

chinois, Chinese

Chinon, red wine from the Loire Valley

chipiron, small squid

chipirons en su tinta, Basque dish of squid cooked in its own ink

chipolatas, small sausages

chips, potato chips

chivry, a *béarnaise* sauce w/spinach, parsley or watercress added to make it green

chocolat, chocolate

chocolat à la bayonne, chocolate cream dessert

chocolat amer, bitter chocolate

chocolat au lait, milk chocolate

chocolat chaud, hot chocolate

chocolat mi-amer, bittersweet chocolate

Hot Chocolate is more common in Europe than in the U.S.

67

chocolat noir, bitter chocolate/black chocolate

choix, "choice." On a menu, this means you can choose among a list of dishes

chope, large beer

choron, *béarnaise* sauce w/tomatoes

chou, cabbage

chou à la crème, cream puff

choucroute, sauerkraut. In Alsace, this refers to a dish of cabbage w/pork, potatoes & sauerkraut

Love choucroute garni!

choucroute garnie, sauerkraut w/ham, pork sausage or frankfurters

Mon petit chou is a term of endearment.

chouée, buttered cabbage dish

chou-fleur, cauliflower

chou frisé, kale/savoy cabbage

chou marin, kale

chou rouge, red cabbage

chou vert, green cabbage

choux de Bruxelles, brussels sprouts

ciboule, scallion

ciboulette, chive

cidre, cider. Popular in Brittany

cigales, a type of clam

cigarette, sugar cookie (rolled in the shape of a cigarette)

citron, the term for lemons & limes (citrus fruit) but can also simply refer to a lemon

citronelle, lemon grass

citronnade, lemon drink

citron pressé, fresh lemon juice w/sugar & water (lemonade)

citron vert, lime

citrouille, pumpkin

civelles, baby eels

civet, game stew. Popular in Corsica

civet de lapin, rabbit stew

civet de lièvre, hare stew

clafouti, fruit baked in pancake batter

LOVE this

clafouti du limousin, cherry *clafouti*

claires, oysters (raised in an oyster bed)

clamart, stuffed w/green peas

Claret, dry, red table wine from Bordeaux

clémentine, seedless tangerine

clos, vineyard

clou de girofle, clove

clouté, "studded with"

cocaos, cocoa

cochon, pig

cochon de lait, suckling pig — *Cochon.*

cochon de lait en gelée, suckling pig in aspic — *I'll pass.*

cochonnailles, assorted pork sausages & pâtés

cocotte, casserole — *Cocotte.*

coeur, heart

coeur d'artichaut, artichoke heart

coeur de filet, thickest & best part of a beef filet

coeurs de palmiers, hearts of palm served w/a mustard vinaigrette

cognac, cognac

coing, quince

Cointreau, orange-flavored liqueur

colbert, à la, dipped in batter & breadcrumbs & fried

colin, hake

colonel, lemon sherbet w/vodka

colvert, wild duck

complet, full/whole

compote, stewed fruit

compote de..., stewed

compris, included

comté, a mild cheese (similar to the Swiss gruyère cheese)

concassé, chopped

concentré, concentrate

concombre, cucumber

concorde, chocolate meringue & chocolate mousse

condiments, seasoning

confiserie, candy & sweets shop

confit, goose, pork, turkey or duck preserved in fat.
   Also vegetables/fruit preserved in alcohol, sugar or vinegar

confiture, jam/preserves.
   Confiture d'oignons is onion compote

confiture de vieux garçon, fruit served in alcohol

confiture d' orange, marmalade

congre, conger eel

consommation, drinks

consommé, broth (clear soup)

Vieux Garçon means Old boy. Something like old maid.

consommé aux vermicelles, broth w/thin noodles
consommé Célestine, broth w/chicken & noodles
consommé colbert, broth w/vegetables & poached eggs
consommé madrilène, cold broth w/tomatoes
consommé princesse, broth w/chicken & asparagus
consultez aussi l'ardoise, other suggestions
    on the blackboard
consultez notre carte des desserts, consult our dessert menu
contre-filet, sirloin
copeaux, shavings (of vegetables or chocolate)
copieux, filling
coppa, fillet (in Corsica)
coq, rooster
coq au vin, chicken stewed in red wine
    w/bacon, onions, mushrooms & herbs
coq de bruyère, grouse
coque, tiny shellfish (similar to a clam)
coquelet, cockerel
coquillage, shellfish
coquille, shell/scallop
coquille Saint-Jacques, scallops (prepared w/a
    parsley butter or a cream sauce)
coquilles à la nantaise, scallops w/onions.
    A specialty in Brittany
corail, the egg sac of lobster,
    crayfish or scallops
corbeille, basket
corbeille de fruits, basket of assorted fruits
cordon bleu, veal slices stuffed w/ham &
    gruyere, breaded & fried in butter
coriandre, coriander
cornet de frites, paper cone filled
    w/french fries. A popular snack
cornets de murat, cones filled w/cream
cornichon, small pickle (gherkin)
corniottes, cheese pastries made in the shape of hats
corps, refers to the "body" of wine
corsoise, à la, this means that the dish is prepared
    as it would be in Corsica
cosse, pod/husk
côte, rib/chop

Coq au vin.
gotta have
it in
Paris

Coquille.

Corbeille.

côte d'agneau, lamb chop

Côte de Beaune, red & white wines from Beaune in Burgundy

côte de boeuf, beef rib steak/T-bone steak

Côte de Nuits, a heavy red Burgundy wine

côte de veau, veal chop

côtelette, cutlet/chop

côtelette d'agneau, lamb chop

côtelette de porc, pork chop

Côtes du Rhône, wine region producing wines such as
    Châteauneuf-du-Pape, Côte-Rotie, Hermitage & *Tavel*

côtes levées, spareribs

cotignac, caramelized apple tart

cotriade, fish stew (from Brittany)

cou, neck

cou d'oie farci, a "sausage" made of the neck skin of a goose
    which is stuffed w/meat & spices

couennes de porc, fresh pork rinds

coulibiac, salmon *pâté*

coulis, vegetable, shellfish or fruit purée

coulis de tomates, thick tomato sauce

coulommiers, a mild cheese (similar to *brie*)

coupe, goblet/scoop/a dish used for serving dessert

coupe Danemark, a scoop of vanilla ice
    cream covered w/hot chocolate sauce

coupe de champagne, a flute of champagne

coupe des îles, a scoop of vanilla ice cream
    w/fruit & whipped cream

Coupe de Champagne.

coupe glacée, ice cream dessert (often a sundae)

courge, squash

courgette, zucchini

courgettes au broccio, *broccio* cheese-stuffed
    zucchini dish from Corsica

couronne, circle-shaped or ring-shaped bread

Couronne means crown or wreath.

court bouillon, seafood broth

couscous, Moroccan specialty of steamed grain, broth, meats,
    vegetables & other ingredients

couscous royal, *couscous* w/meat

cousinat, bean, bell pepper, artichoke, tomato, green onion &
    carrot dish

couteau, knife

Couteau - coo.toe.

couvert, cover charge/place setting

couvert, vin et service compris, the price includes wine, tip & cover charge

crabe, crab

crabe verte, shore crab

crapaudine, grilled game or poultry dish

craquelins, cookies

Crécy, à la, served w/carrots

crème, cream/creamy soup/creamy dessert. Can also refer to sweet liqueur as in *crème de menthe*. *À la crème* means served w/a cream sauce

crème à la vanille, vanilla custard

crème allégée, light cream

crème anglaise, custard

crème brûlée, custard dessert topped w/caramelized sugar

crème caramel, vanilla custard w/caramel sauce

crème catalane, caramel-covered trifle w/cinnamon & anise

crème champignons, cream of mushroom soup

crème chantilly, vanilla-flavored & sweetened whipped cream

crème d'asperges, cream of asparagus soup

crème de cacao, cocoa-flavored liqueur

crème de cassis, black currant liqueur

crème de marrons, chestnut purée

crème de menthe, mint-flavored liqueur

crème de poireaux, cream of leek soup

crème de poulet, cream of chicken soup

crème de volaille, cream of chicken soup

crème épaisse, heavy cream

crème fouettée, whipped cream

crème fraîche, thick, heavy cream

crème frit, fried cream custard dessert from Burgundy

crème glacée, ice cream

crème pâtissière, custard filling in cakes & pastry

crème plombières, custard filled w/fresh fruit

crème renversée, custard dessert in a mold

crèmerie, store selling dairy products

cremets, cream made in molds w/fruit

crêpe, crepe (thin pancake). Popular in Brittany

crêpe froment, buckwheat crepe w/sweet filling

crêpe Suzette, crepe w/orange sauce, flamed w/orange liqueur

crépine, caul fat (fat covering the intestines) used to wrap *pâtés* & *terrines*

We like anything with crème attached.

crépinette, small sausage patty wrapped in caul fat
cresson, watercress
cressonade, watercress sauce
cressonière, watercress soup
crête de coq, cock's comb *YES, they eat*
    (the fleshy crest on the head of fowl) *this.*
creuse, a type of oyster
crevette, shrimp
crevette grise, gray, small shrimp
crevette rose, red shrimp w/firm flesh
cristallisés, crystallized
crist-marine, algae
croissant, crescent-shaped flaky breakfast
    roll made of flour, eggs & butter
croquant, crispy
croquants, crispy honey or almond cookies
croque madame, toasted ham &
    cheese sandwich topped w/an egg   *Croquembouche.*
croquembouche, cream-puff tree   *Typically served*
croque monsieur, toasted ham   *at weddings.*
    & cheese sandwich
croquette, ground meat, fish or vegetables
    coated in bread crumbs & deep fried
crosse, shank
crottin/croutin de chavignol, a firm
    goat cheese
croustade, pie filled w/meat, seafood &/or vegetables
croustillant, crisp/spicy
croûte, crust   *Yes, please.*
croûte au fromage, melted cheese served on a slice of toast
croûte de sel, en, in a salt crust
croûte, en, in a pastry crust
croûte forestière, mushrooms on toast
croûtes, croutons
croûton, small toasted piece of bread, usually served in a salad
cru, raw. On a wine list, this means vintage
cru classé, high-quality wine
crudités, raw vegetables   *cuiller ~*
crustacé, shellfish (crustaceans)   *Qui-air*
cuiller, spoon
cuillère, à la, a dish eaten w/a spoon

cuisine, there are four categories of French cuisine:

> *Cuisine campagnarde* (also known as
> > *cuisine des provinces*):
> > > Traditional regional dishes prepared
> > > with fresh ingredients.
>
> *Cuisine bourgeoise*: French home cooking.
> *Haute cuisine*: An elaborate meal with many
> > courses featuring
> > rich and fresh ingredients.
>
> *Nouvelle cuisine*: Light sauces and small portions that
> > emphasize the colors and textures of the ingredients.

cuisse, leg & thigh (denotes dark meat)

cuisse de poulet, chicken drumstick w/thigh

cuisses de grenouilles, frogs' legs

cuissot, haunch of game or veal

Cuisse ~
Kweece
is dark
meat

cuit, cooked

cuit à la vapeur, steamed

cuit au four, baked

cul, haunch

cul de veau, veal pot roast

culotte, rump

cumin, cumin

curaçao, orange-flavored liqueur

curcuma, the spice turmeric (used in curry powder)

cure-dent, (served w/a) toothpick

currie/curry, curry

cuvée, blend of wines or champagne/house wine

Cynar, aperitif w/an artichoke base

darne, thick fillet of fish (often salmon)

dartois, pastry w/jam

datte, date

daube, stew

daube à la niçoise, beef or lamb stew w/red wine,
tomatoes & onions

daube de boeuf, beef stew

daube provençal, gravy w/capers, garlic & anchovies

dauphinois, a mild cheese

daurade, white fish (usually served grilled) found in the South
of France (sea bream)

déca, decaf   *déca ~ day-cah*

décaféiné, decaffeinated

décortiqué, shelled/peeled

déglacée, warmed up

dégustation, sampling/tasting

déjeuner, lunch

délice, a delight/a treat

délimité de qualité supérieure, on a wine bottle, this means a superior-quality wine

demi, half/small beer

demi-bouteille, half bottle

demi-deuil, usually means served w/truffles

demidoff, w/vegetables

demi-glace, beef-stock sauce

demi-sel, soft, salty cream cheese/salted butter

demi-sec, medium dry

demoiselle de Cherbourg, small lobster

denté, dentex (fish)

désossé, boned

dessert, dessert

diable, hot, spicy sauce (often, a strong mustard sauce)/devilled.) This is also the term for an unglazed, porous pot used to cook vegetables

diabolo, a drink usually mixed w/lemonade

diane, a brown sauce w/vinegar & peppercorns

dieppoise, shrimp & mussels served in a white wine sauce

digestif, after-dinner drink

dijonnaise, served w/mustard

dinde, turkey

dindon, turkey

dindonneau, young turkey

dîner, dinner

diplomate, custard dessert w/spongecake, crystallized fruit & topped w/liqueur

discrétion, when you see this on a menu, it means that you can drink as much wine as you want (for a fixed price)

divine, *hollandaise* sauce w/sherry

dodine de canard, stuffed-duck dish

domaine, on a wine label this notes a high-quality wine

dorade, Mediterranean sea bass

demi-bouteille ~
deh-mee-
boo-tay

dinde ~ dand
dindon ~ dan-dong
dindonea ~ dandon-oh

doré(e), golden

dos, back

dos et ventre, both sides (means "back & front")

douce, sweet

doucette, salad green (a cousin of *mâche*)

douceurs, desserts

doux, mild, sweet

douzaine, dozen

dragées, candied almonds

Dubonnet, wine & brandy-based aperitif w/herbs

duchesse, potatoes mixed w/egg & forced through a pastry tube

dugléré, a white sauce w/tomatoes, shallots & white wine

duxelles, finely chopped sautéed mushrooms

eau, water

eau au syphon, w/seltzer water

eau avec gaz, carbonated water

eau de source, spring water

eau-de-vie, brandy made from distilled fruit juice. Sold in elaborate tall & thin bottles in Alsace. The term means "water of life." This can also refer to any spirit

Don't worry you can drink the water in France.

eau du robinet, tap water

eau glacée, iced water

eau minérale, mineral water

eau minérale gazeuse, carbonated mineral water

eau nature, tap water

eau plate, still (not sparkling) water

eau sans gaz, water w/out carbonation

écailler, oyster opener/fish scaler

échalote, shallot

échine, spareribs

éclair, pastry filled w/vanilla custard & topped w/chocolate icing

écrevisse, crayfish

écrevisse à la nage, crayfish in a white wine sauce

édam français, nutty-flavored, orange-colored cheese originally from the Netherlands

édulcorant, artificial sweetener

effilée, thinly sliced

Ecrevisse.

effiloché, thinly sliced

églefin, haddock

emballé, wrapped

embeurré, buttered/buttery

embeurrée de chou, buttered cabbage

émincé, slices of cooked meat in gravy/anything thinly sliced

émincé de veau, sauteed veal slices w/creme sauce

emmental, Swiss cheese

emporter, à, take-out foods

émulsionné, liquified

Sounds good. Never had it.

enchaud de porc à la périgourdine, pork loin stuffed ←
  w/truffles. A specialty in Southwest France

encornet, small squid

endive, endive/chicory

enrubanne, layered dish
  (looks like ribbons)

entier, whole

entrecôte, rib-eye steak

entrecôte Bercy, steak w/wine sauce

Endive.

entrecôte maître d'hôtel, rib-eye steak served w/herb butter

entrecôte marchand de vin, rib-eye steak served in
  red wine sauce

Entre-Deux-Mers, a region of Bordeaux
  that produces white wine

entrée, first course/appetizer

entremets, dessert

épaule, shoulder

épeautre, a variety of wheat

éperlan, smelt

épice, spice

épicé, peppered/spicy

épicerie, small grocery store

épi de maïs, miniature corn
  on the cob (often pickled)

épinard, spinach

ÉPICERIE

Be sure to visit a grocery store ~ small or large, they're worth the trip.

épinards en branches, leaf spinach

époisse, a cow's-milk cheese from Burgundy

érable, maple

escabèche, raw fish marinated in lime juice & herbs. In
  Provence, this can refer to a cold marinated sardine dish

escalope, scallop/cutlet

escalope de veau, veal scallop

escalope panée, breaded veal scallop

escalope viennoise, breaded veal
   cutlet (weiner schnitzel)

escargot, snail

escargot de mer, sea snail

escargot petit-gris, small snail

escarole, a type of *endive*

espadon, swordfish

Escargot.

essence, essence

estocaficada, cod stew

estofat de boeuf, beef stew

estouffade, beef stew. Can also refer to a steamed dish

estouffados, almond butter cookies found in Provence

estragon, tarragon

esturgeon, sturgeon

et, and

Estragon.

étrille, small crab

étouffée, stewed

étuvé/étuvée, steamed

éventail, en, cut into a fan shape

express, espresso

extra-sec, very dry (champagne)

façon, in the manner of

faisan

faisan, pheasant

faisan normand, pheasant w/apples & *calvados*

faisselle, fresh cow's-milk cheese

fait à la maison, homemade

falette, stuffed breast of veal

far, prune tart

farandole, dessert &/or cheese cart

farce, spiced ground meat (usually pork) used for stuffing

farci, stuffed, as in *chou farci* (stuffed cabbage)
   & *tomates farcies* (stuffed tomatoes).
   In Nice, this is a dish of ⟵ *love these*
   stuffed vegetables

farigoule, the name in Provence for wild thyme

farine, flour

farine de blé, wheat flour

farine de maïs, corn flour

faux-filet, flank steak/sirloin steak

fécule, starch. ***Fécule de pommes de terre*** is potato flour used to thicken sauces & soups

fécule de maïs, cornstarch

fendant, "melting." Refers to extremely tender meat or chocolate

fenouil, fennel

féra, dace (lake salmon)

ferme, farm/farm fresh

fermier, poultry raised on a farm

feu de bois, cooked on a wood fire

feuille, leaf

feuille de chêne, oak-leaf lettuce

feuille de laurel, bay leaf

feuille de vigne, vine leaf

feuilles farcies, grape leaves stuffed w/rice & herbs

feuilletage, puff pastry

feuilletée, puff pastry

fève, broad bean

fiadone, cheesecake found in Corsica

ficelle, small baguette. *Ficellé* means tied w/a string

figatelli, Corsican liver sausage

figue, fig

figue de barbarie, prickly pear

filet, fillet

filet à la mistral, filet of sole w/tomatoes & mushrooms

filet de boeuf, beef fillet

filet de boeuf à la Poitou, beef fillet w/chicken liver *pâté*

filet de boeuf Bordelaise, beef fillet in a red wine sauce

filet de sole, fillet of sole

filet de sole meunière, fillet of sole fried in butter

filet doria, fillet of sole w/cucumbers

filet mignon, small round beef tenderloin fillet

filet Saint-Germain, fillet of sole w/potatoes

financière, cream & Madeira wine sauce. This can also refer to a dish w/veal or chicken dumplings

fine, a fine brandy

fines de claire, oysters

fines herbes, mixture of herbs (such as parsley, chives, tarragon & thyme)

flageolets, small kidney-shaped beans

flagnarde/flaugnarde, fruit-filled cake

[handwritten note:] Feu de bois on a sign outside a restaurant indicates that they cook with wood.

[handwritten note:] ficelle means string.

[handwritten note:] figues.

flamande, à la, "Flemish style" w/potatoes, stuffed cabbage
leaves, vegetables, sausage & bacon

flambé(e), flaming

flamiche, savory tart (similar to a quiche)

flan, tart or crustless pie. Can also refer to the caramel custard
dessert of the same name found in Spain

flanchet, flank

flet, flounder

flétan, halibut

fleur, flower. *Fleurs* are crystallized flowers used on desserts

fleurette, small flower

Fleurie, a red wine from Beaujolais

fleurons, crescent-shaped puff pastries

fleurs de courgettes farcies, zucchini flowers stuffed w/cheese

flocon, flake

flocons d'avoine, oat flakes

florentine, w/spinach

foie, liver

foie de veau, calf's liver

foie de veau grand-mère, sautéed calf's liver w/bacon,
onion & potato garnish

foie de volaille, chicken liver

foie gras, fattened goose liver

foie gras de canard, fattened duck liver

foie gras d'oie, fattened goose liver

foie gras en brioche, fattened goose liver that is marinated &
cooked & baked a second time in a pastry shell

foies blonds de volaille, chicken livers

foin, cooked in hay ⟵ *I'd rather not.*

fond, bottom

fondant, cake icing

fondant au chocolat, similar to a brownie (but better!)

fond d'artichaut, artichoke heart

fondu/fondue (au fromage), melted cheese in a pot. Dip your
bread or meat in!

fondu aux raisins, the crust of this smooth & creamy cheese is
made of grape pulp. Also known as *tomme au marc*

fondue bourguignonne, small pieces of meat dipped into
oil & eaten w/sauces

fondue chinoise, thin slices of beef dipped in bouillon
& eaten w/sauces

fondue savoyarde, pot of melted cheese for dipping

forestière, ("forester's style") usually means w/sautéed mushrooms

forêt noire, Black Forest cake

forme d'Ambert, a blue cheese

formule, une, a set-price menu

fort, strong (as in strong or sharp cheese)

fougasse, decorated bread loaf w/olive oil flavoring & sometimes w/bacon, onion or tomato stuffing

fougassette, a slice of *brioche* bread flavored w/orange & saffron

four, au, baked

fourchette, fork

fournée, baked

fournitures, fresh herbs & salad greens

fourré, filled/stuffed

fraîche, fresh

frais, fresh

fraise, strawberry

[handwritten notes: Fraîche - fraysh / Frais - fray / Fraise - frez]

fraise des bois, wild strawberry

framboise, raspberry/raspberry liqueur

frangipane, almond custard filling

frappé, drink blended w/ice

frémis, oysters (served almost raw)

friand, meat-filled pastry

friandises, *petits fours*

fricadelles, fried meat patties

fricadelles à la bière, meatballs in beer. A specialty in Belgium

fricandeau, braised veal dish

fricassée, a stew of meat, poultry or fish finished w/cream

fricassée liégeoise, fried eggs, bacon & sausage. A specialty in Belgium

frigolet, name in Provence for wild thyme

frisée, curly endive

frit, fried

fritelli, chestnut-flour doughnuts from Corsica

frites, french fries (often eaten w/mayonnaise) *[handwritten: ← yes!]*

fritons, minced spread made of organ meats *[handwritten: ← No!]*

fritot, batter fried or fritter

friture, frying

friture de mer/friture de poisson, fried small fish

froid, cold   *Froid ~ Fwa*

fromage, cheese. It is said that
   there are over 400 different French cheeses

fromage à pâte dure, hard cheese

fromage à pâte molle, soft cheese

fromage au marc, a sharp, tangy cheese   *I don't*

fromage blanc, cream cheese (but runny)   *think so.*

fromage de brebis, sheep's-milk cheese

fromage de chèvre, goat's-milk cheese

fromage de tête, headcheese (sausage made from the meat of a
   calf's or pig's head cooked in a gelatinous meat
   broth & then served cold)

fromage fermier, cheese made where the milk is produced

fromage fort, extremely soft cheese from Provence mixed
   w/herbs, salt, pepper & *marc*

fromage maigre, low-fat cheese

fromagerie, cheese shop

fruit, fruit   *Fruit ~ fru-ee*

fruit confit, candied fruit

fruit de la passion, passion fruit

fruits de mer, seafood

fumé, smoked

fumet, fish stock

galantine, cold gelatinized meat dish

galette, buckwheat pancake. *Galettes de blé de sarrasin* are
   crêpes made w/dark flour and filled w/cheese, ham,
   an egg, mushrooms or any number of things.
   Galettes de blé de froment are dessert crêpes made with
   light flour. *Galettè* can also refer to a flaky pastry "cake"
   w/an almond paste filling. This is the traditional cake served
   on Three Kings' Day. A bean (now a little porcelain statue is
   used) is put in the cake & the person who gets the piece
   containing the bean is king or queen for the day & wears a
   a gold crown

galette bretonne, butter & rum cake

galette de pommes, apple tart

galette de sarrasin, buckwheat pancake w/savoury filling
   popular in Brittany

galopin, bread pancake

Gamay de Touraine, red wine made w/the Gamay grape

gambas, large prawns

gambas à la planxa, grilled shrimp served on a plank of wood
ganses, fried cakes topped w/sugar
garbure, cabbage soup. In Southern France, this is usually
　　cabbage soup w/ham
garni(e), w/vegetables/garnished
garniture, vegetables/garnished
gâteau, cake
gâteau au chocolat, chocolate cake
gâteau au fromage, cheese tart
gâteau de Savoie, spongecake
gâteau de riz, rice pudding

gateau ~ gat-oh

gaufre, waffle. A specialty in Belgium
gaufrette, sweet wafer
gayettes, small sausage patties
gazeuse, carbonated.
　　Non-gazeuse means not carbonated
gelé, frozen
gelée, jellied/in aspic
gélinotte, prairie chicken
genièvre, juniper berry
génoise, spongecake
germiny, sorrel & cream soup/w/sorrel

gelée. Hmmm. not something we eat with gusto.

gésier, gizzard
Gewürztraminer, dry white wine from Alsace
gibelotte de lapin, rabbit stew
gibier, game
gigot, leg
gigot d'agneau, leg of lamb
gigot de mer, oven-roasted monkfish dish
gigot de mouton pré-salé, leg of lamb dish made w/lambs
　　that graze in salt meadows in Northwest France
gigot farci, stuffed leg of lamb
gigue, the haunch of game meat
gimblettes, ring cookies
gin, gin
gingembre, ginger
gin tonique, gin & tonic
girofle, clove
girolle, chanterelle mushroom
glaçage, frosting
glace, ice/ice cream

glacé, iced/glazed

glace à la napolitaine, layers of different-flavored ice cream

glace au fondant, shiny cake icing

glace crémeuse, ice cream

glace de viande, concentrated meat stock (meat glaze)

glace de poisson, concentrated fish stock

glaçons, ice

globe, round (cut of meat)

gnocchi, gnocchi (potato dumplings). Found frequently on menus in Nice & near the Italian border

gnocchi aux blettes, gnocchi w/Swiss chard incorporated into the dough

gougère, cheese-flavored pastry ← *Oui, s'il vous plaît.*

goujon, gudgeon (related to carp)

goujonnettes, small slices of fish

gourmandises, sweets/candies

gousse, clove

gousse d'ail, clove of garlic

goûter, snack/to taste

graine, grain/seed

graine de maïs, corn meal

graine de moutarde, mustard seed

graines de paradis, similar to the spice cardamom & found in the former French African colonies

graisse, fat

graisserons, fried pieces of goose or duck skin *Graisserons. These are like cracklings and used as garnish.*

grand, large

grand crème, a large milky coffee

grand cru, high-quality wine

Grand Marnier, orange liqueur

grand-mère, means "grandmother." A garnish usually of mushrooms, potatoes & bacon

grand veneur, brown sauce w/red currants (usually served w/game)

grand vin, high-quality wine

granité, slushy iced drink

gras, fat/fatty

gras-double, tripe simmered in wine & onions

gratin, au, topped w/grated cheese, breadcrumbs & butter & then baked

gratin dauphinois, potato au gratin dish w/eggs, cheese & cream

gratin de fruits de mer, shellfish in a cream sauce

gratin de queues d'écrevisses, freshwater crayfish served *au gratin*

gratin de capucins, *gratin* of stuffed artichoke hearts

gratin savoyard, baked sliced-potato casserole

gratiné, prepared w/breadcrumbs

gratinée, topped w/cheese/onion soup

grattons, fried pieces of pork, goose or duck skin

gratuit, free

Graves, wine region of Bordeaux

grecque, cold vegetable mixture (*légumes à la grecque*). *À la grecque* refers to dishes stewed in oil (in the Greek style)

grelot, small white onion

grenade, pomegranate

grenadin, small veal scallop

grenoblois, caramel-walnut cake

grenouille, frog

gribiche, mayonnaise w/gherkins & capers. *Sauce gribiche* can refer to a vinaigrette & egg sauce

grillade, grilled meat/mixed grill

grillé, grilled

griotte, a type of cherry (usually in white alcohol)

Grenouille.

grive, thrush (a bird)

grondin, spiked-headed ocean fish (gurnet)

gros bout de poitrine, brisket

groseille, currant

groseille à maquereau, gooseberry/currant

groseille rouge, red currant

gros sel, coarse salt

grumes, heavy coating or skin

Gruyère

gruyère, Swiss cheese

guimauve, marshmallow

haché, hashed

hachis, hash

hachis parmentier, shepherd's pie (ground meat & mashed potatoes topped w/a white sauce & served in a casserole)

hareng, herring

harengs fumés à la Créole, spicy smoked herring dish flamed in rum (found in the French West Indies)

haricot, bean

haricot de mer, tiny clam

haricot de mouton, mutton, bean & potato stew

haricot de soisson, navy bean/kidney bean

haricot rouge, red kidney bean

Haricots.

haricots en salade, bean salad

haricots verts, green beans (french beans)

Henri IV, artichoke hearts & *béarnaise* sauce

herbes, herbs

herbes de Provence, mixture of herbs that includes fennel, lavender, marjoram, bay leaf, sage, rosemary & thyme

hérisson de mer, sea urchin

hochepot, oxtail stew *We like the name.*

hollandaise, sauce of melted butter, egg yolks & lemon juice

homard, lobster

homard à l'américaine, flaming lobster dish w/white wine, herbs, tomatoes & garlic

homard à l'armoricaine, lobster in a tomato sauce

homard cardinal, flaming lobster dish w/mushrooms & truffles

homard froid à la parisienne, cold lobster garnished w/diced vegetables in a mayonnaise sauce

homard Newburg, lobster cooked in a sauce made of butter, cream, wine (or brandy) & egg yolks

homard Thermidor, flaming lobster dish w/white wine, herbs, spices & mustard

hongroise, served w/paprika & cream (means "Hungarian")

hors-d'oeuvre, appetizer

huile, oil

huile d'arachide, peanut oil

Hors d'oeuvre. means without work.

huile de carthame, safflower oil

huile de noix, walnut oil

huile de soya, soybean oil

huile de tournesol, sunflower oil

huile d'olive (vierge), olive oil (virgin)

huître, oyster

huître belon, pink oyster

huître portugaise, Portuguese lobster (small & fat)

hure de porc, pig's head

hure de saumon, salmon pâté

hysope, the bitter herb hysop

île flottante, meringues floating in a cream sauce

impératrice, rice-pudding dessert

importée, imported

indienne, w/curry (in the style of India)

infusion, herbal tea

jalousies, apricot pastry

jambe, leg

jambon, ham

jambon à l'os, baked ham

jambon blanc, boned, cooked ham

jambon cuit, cooked ham

jambon cuit d'Ardennes, smoked ham found in Belgium

jambon de Bayonne, raw, salty ham

jambon de canard, cured, salted or smoked duck or goose breast

jambon de montagne, local cured ham

jambon de Paris, lightly salted ham

jambon de Parme, Parma ham (prosciutto)

jambon de pays, local "country" cured ham

jambon de York, smoked ham (English style)

jambon d'oie, cured, salted or smoked duck or goose breast

jambon cru, cured ham

jambonneau, pork knuckle

jambon persillé, parsleyed ham

jardinière, w/diced vegetables

jarret, shank/knuckle

jarret de veau, veal shank (usually a stew)

jerez, sherry (Spanish for sherry)

Jésus de Morteau, smoked pork sausage

jeune, young/green (as in unripe)

joue, cheek

jour, du, of the day

jud mat gardebóneh, smoked pork & bean dish found in Luxembourg

julienne, vegetables cut into fine strips. There is also a fish w/this name

jumeau, pot roast

Handwritten notes:

île flottante... don't see the appeal of this but it's very popular.

à l'os means bone-in.

← Never warmed up to this

87

Jura, one of France's wine-growing regions
jus, juice/gravy
jus de tomate, tomato juice
jus d'orange, orange juice
kaki, persimmon
kalouga, chocolate-pudding cake
ketchup, ketchup
kig-ha-farz, buckwheat pudding
    w/vegetables & meat

Jus d'orange is usually served with water and sugar.

kir, apéritif made w/*crème de cassis* & wine
kir royal, apéritif made w/champagne & *crème de cassis*
kirsch, cherry-flavored liqueur
kougelhopf/kouglof/kugelhopf, Alsatian cake w/raisins
    & almonds
kouigh amann, buttered pastry
l', la, le, the (singular). *Les* is the (plural)
lait, milk
laitance, fish roe
lait de beurre, buttermilk
lait écrémé, skim milk
lait entier, whole milk
laitue, lettuce
lambi, conch found in the French West Indies
lamelle, very thin slice
lamproie, lamprey

Lamproie — yikes.

langouste, crayfish
langouste à la sètoise, lobster (crawfish) w/garlic, tomatoes &
    cognac
langoustine, prawn
langue, tongue

Langue de chat means cat's tongue.

langue de chat, biscuit & ice-cream dessert
Languedoc, one of France's wine-growing regions
languedocienne, usually means eggplant,
    tomato & mushroom garnish
lapereau, young rabbit
lapin, rabbit
lapin à l'artésienne, rabbit stew
lapin à la Lorraine, rabbit in a
    mushroom & cream sauce
lapin aux pruneaux, rabbit w/prunes.
    A popular dish in Northern France

Lapin sworn enemy of all gardeners.

lapin chasseur, rabbit in a white wine & herb sauce

lapin de garenne, wild rabbit

lapin en paquets, rabbit pieces in a packet
of bacon. A specialty in Provence

lard, bacon

lardon, diced bacon

laurier, bay leaf

Laurier.

lavande, lavender. Lavender blossoms are added to dishes in
Provence such as *sorbet de lavande* (lavender sorbet)

lèche, thin slice (usually of meat or bread)

léger, light

légère, light (as in light beer)

légumes, vegetables

lentilles, lentils

levraut, young rabbit

levure, yeast

libre service, self-service

lieu, small saltwater fish

lièvre, rabbit (hare)

lièvre en cabessal, stuffed hare dish

limande, dab (flounder)

limande sole, lemon sole

limonade, lemonade-flavored soft drink

Limonade is a carbonated soft drink.

liqueur, liqueur

lisette, small mackerel

lit, bed (as in a bed of lettuce)

litre, liter. Wine is often served in a liter carafe, *demi-litre*
(half-liter) or *un quart* (quarter-liter)

livarot, round, sharp, tangy cheese

Loire, this valley is one of France's wine regions along the
Loire River

longe, loin

longe de veau, loin of veal

longeole, pork sausage stuffed w/cabbage, leeks & spinach.
A specialty in French-speaking Switzerland

lonzu, shoulder (in Corsica)

lorraine, usually braised in red wine w/cabbage

lotte, monkfish

loubine, fish similar to sea bass

lou cachat, crushed cheese

lou magret, breast of fattened goose or duck

Lou means "the" in Provençal!

lou mäis, corn-meal cake found in Provence

loup, sea bass

loup au fenouille, sea bass grilled over fennel stalks

loup de mer, sea bass

lou pevre, goat's-milk cheese w/coarsely ground pepper

lou piech, stuffed veal dish found around Nice

louvine, fish similar to sea bass

Lucullus, refers to any dish that contains extremely rich &/or rare ingredients. Named after a Roman general who hosted great feasts

lyonnaise, sautéed w/mushrooms &/or onions/sauce of onions, butter & white wine ("Lyon style")

macaron, macaroon

macaroni au gratin, macaroni & cheese

macédoine, mixed fruit or mixed vegetables

macédoine de légumes, mixed vegetables

macérer, to pickle or soak

mâche, a type of lettuce

macis, the outer covering of a nutmeg/mace

mache.

Mâcon, wine from Burgundy

mâconnaise, usually refers to a goat's milk cheese

macreuse, pot roast

madeleine, butter cake

madère, w/Madeira wine

magret, breast of fattened goose or duck

maigre, lean

maïs, corn

maison, house

maître d'hôtel, head waiter/sautéed in butter w/lemon juice & parsley

maltaise, orange-flavored *hollandaise* sauce

mandarine, tangerine

mange-tout, snow pea/type of apple

mangue, mango

manière, de, in the style of

maquereau, mackerel

mange-tout means eat all

maraîchère, usually means w/various greens (market style)

marbré, marbled

marc, a strong liqueur made from distilling the residue of grapes (similar to Italian *grappa*). **Marc de Bandol** is a popular *marc* found in Provence

marcassin, young wild boar

marchand de vin, red wine & shallot sauce/wine merchant

marché, market

marée, a term used to denote fresh seafood (literally "the tide")

Marengo, à la, w/eggs

marennes, flat-shelled oysters

margarine, margarine (almost never served in Paris)

Margaux, a red wine from Bordeaux

mariné, marinated

marinière, "sailor's style" usually means w/seafood (most often mussels) simmered in herbs & white wine

marjolaine, marjoram. This can also refer to a layered chocolate & nut cake

marmelade, marmalade

marmite, food cooked in a small casserole

marquise, mousse cake

maroilles, strong, hard cheese

marron, chestnut

marrons au sirop, chestnuts in vanilla-flavored syrup

marrons chauds, roasted chestnuts. Served on the streets of Paris

marrons entiers au naturel, chestnuts in water (used in stuffing, sauces or as a vegetable)

marrons glacés, candied chestnuts

marrons Mont Blanc, chestnut purée & cream on a spongecake soaked in rum

massepain, marzipan

matafan, simple cake (flour, butter, milk & eggs) made in a skillet

matelote, freshwater fish stew/fish stew (usually eel) w/wine from the French West Indies. ***Matelote de veau*** is veal stew w/red wine

mauresque, a drink of *pastis* w/almond & orange syrup

mauviette, meadow lark

mayonnaise, mayonnaise

médaillon, small, round cut of meat

Médoc, red wine from Bordeaux

mélange, mixture/blend

mélasses, molasses

méli-mélo, assorted seafood

méli-mélo de légumes, mixed vegetables

Marquise... don't miss having this.

marrons ~ have never seen the appeal of these.

melon, cantaloupe

melon à l'italienne, melon w/*prosciutto*

melon d'eau, watermelon. The French call it ***pastèque***

melon de Cavaillon, similar to a canteloupe

ménagère, a basic preparation usually w/carrots, potatoes &/or onions (means "in the style of a housewife")

mendiants, dessert made of dry figs, raisins, almonds & nuts

menthe, mint

menthe poivrée, peppermint

menu, menu (often a fixed-price meal)

menu dégustation, set-price gourmet menu of specialties of the chef

Menu degustation is usually better Quality.

menu du jour, menu of the day

menu fixe, fixed-price menu

menu gastronomique, gourmet menu

menu pour enfant, children's menu

mer, sea

merda, *gnocchi* made w/Swiss chard

merenda, morning snack

merguez, spicy sausage (usually lamb)

meringues, baked shells of sweetened, beaten egg whites

merlan, whiting

merle, blackbird

Merlot, dry, medium- to full-bodied red wine

Merle.

merlu, a type of hake

merluche, dried cod

mérou, grouper

merveille, sugar doughnut

No thanks.

mesclun, lettuce salad of mixed greens

messine, an herb & cream sauce

méthode champenoise, sparkling wine (natural method)

mets, dish/preparation

mets selon la saison, seasonal preparation

meunière, w/parsley butter/seasoned fish floured & fried in butter, lemon & parsley. The word means "miller's wife" which refers to the flour that is used to prepare this dish

meurette, w/red wine sauce

Meursault, wine from Burgundy

miel, honey

miel Lavan

miettes, flakes/crumbs

mignardises, *petits fours* (small fancy cookies or cakes)
mignon, tenderloin cut
mignonette, small piece of fillet/coarsely ground white pepper
mijoté, simmered
milieu de poitrine, brisket
millas, corn-meal mush
mille-feuille, light pastry w/cream filling (napoleon)
millésime, vintage
mimolette, a mild cheese
mimosa, w/chopped egg yolks
mirabeau, w/anchovies & olives
mirabelle, yellow plum/plum brandy
mireilie, à la, there are many versions
    of this cold marinade

Mille feuille means a thousand leaves.

mirepoix, vegetables cut into cubes
miroir pommes, apple-Bavarian cream dessert
miroton, slices. Can also refer to a meat & onion stew or a
    brown sauce including onions
mitonnée, a souplike dish
mixte, mixed
mode, à la, in the style of
moelle, bone/marrow
moelleux, full-bodied. This can also mean tender
moka, coffee
mollusques, shellfish
momie, thimble-sized *pastis*
montagne, de, from the mountains
Mont Blanc, chestnut meringue topped w/a "mountain" of
    whipped cream (named after the mountain peak)
montmorency, w/cherries
morceau, piece
morille, morel mushroom (a rare,
    wild mushroom w/a smoky flavor)

morceau ~ mor-so

mornay, white sauce w/cheese
mortadelle, bologna sausage
    w/pistachios & pickles
morue, salt cod
morue en rayte, cod in red wine sauce
moscovite, a dessert made in a mold w/any number of
    ingredients/a way of preparing duck
mouclade, creamy mussel soup

moule, mussel

moule de bouchot, small cultivated mussel

moule d'Espagne, large sharp-shelled mussel (frequently served raw)

moule de Parques, Dutch cultivated mussel

moules à la crème, mussels in white wine w/cream

moules à la poulette, mussels in a rich white wine sauce

moules marinières, mussels simmered in white wine w/shallots

mourtayrol, chicken dish flavored w/saffron

moussaka, a Greek dish frequently found on menus in Paris. It is an eggplant, lamb & tomato casserole

mousse, a light & airy dish of whipped cream or beaten egg whites/chopped meat or fish w/eggs & cream

mousse au chocolat, chocolate mousse

mousse de foie gras, *foie gras* must have, under French law, fattened liver w/up to 20% other foods. *Mousse de foie gras* contains up to 45% other foods such as eggs, pork liver &/or truffles

mousseline, w/whipped cream/*hollandaise* sauce w/cream

mousseron, small wild mushroom

mousseux, sparkling

moutarde, mustard

mouton, mutton

muge, mullet (in Provence)

mulet, mullet

munster, full-bodied cheese, often flavored w/caraway, cumin or anise)

mûre, blackberry

muscade, nutmeg

Muscadet, a dry, white wine

muscat, dessert wine

museau, muzzle

museau de veau, calf's muzzle

myrtille, blueberry

mystère, cooked meringue dessert w/ice cream

nage, "swimming;" served in an aromatic poaching liquid

nantua, crayfish or shrimp sauce

napolitaine, vanilla, strawberry & chocolate ice cream

nappe, tablecloth

nappé, covered in a sauce

nature, plain

naturel, plain. *Au naturel* means plainly cooked

navarin, mutton stew w/turnips

navet, turnip

nefle, small orange-colored fruit

nègre, flourless chocolate cake

neige, w/beaten egg whites (means "snow")

neufchâtel, rich, creamy cheese (a lower-fat cheese)

Newburg, lobster cooked in a sauce made of butter, cream, wine (or brandy) & egg yolks. Newburg is an alteration of Wenburg, the name of the patron for whom the sauce was named

niçoise, usually means w/tomatoes, anchovies, vinegar & black olives. Named after the city of Nice

nid d'abeilles, honey cake

nivernaise , à la, a dish w/carrots & onions

Noilly Prat, French vermouth

noir, black

noisette, hazelnut/round piece of meat

noix, nut/walnut. This can also refer to nuggets

noix d'acajou, cashew

noix de coco, coconut

noix de muscade, nutmeg

noix de pecan, pecan

noix de veau, top side of the leg of veal

non, not or no

nonats, tiny Mediterranean fish served deep fried

normande, usually means cooked w/fish, cream & mushrooms ("Normandy style"). This can also refer to a dish in a cream sauce often w/*calvados*

nougats, roasted almonds, egg whites, nuts & honey dessert

nouilles, noodles

nouilles fraîches maison, homemade fresh pasta

nouveau, new

nouveauté, new offering

nouvelle, new

noyau, pit (as in an olive pit)

Nuits-Saint-Georges, high-quality red wine from Burgundy

oeuf, egg. *Blancs d'oeufs* are egg whites & *jaunes d'oeufs* are egg yolks

oeuf à la coque, soft-boiled egg

oeuf à l'américaine, fried egg

[handwritten marginalia:] Navarin... I'll pass.

[handwritten marginalia:] abeille~ bee

[handwritten marginalia:] Noisette can also mean a small cup of café crème.

[handwritten marginalia:] Oeuf à la Coque— egg in the shell.

oeuf à la russe, hard-boiled egg served
    cold w/diced vegetables in mayonnaise
oeuf à l'Huguenote, poached egg w/meat sauce
oeuf au plat, fried egg
oeuf brouillé, scrambled egg
oeuf chemise, poached egg
oeuf Côte d'Azur, poached egg in an artichoke bottom
oeuf dur, hard-boiled egg
oeuf dur soubise, hard-boiled egg w/onion & cream sauce
oeuf en gelée, poached egg served in gelatin
oeuf en meurette, poached egg in a red wine sauce
oeuf farci, stuffed egg
oeuf frit, fried egg
oeuf mayonnaise, eggs & mayonnaise
oeuf mollet, soft-boiled egg
oeuf poché, poached egg
oeuf poché à la Chartres, poached egg w/tarragon
oeuf Rossini, egg w/truffles & Madeira wine. This can also be a
    poached egg w/*pâté*
oeufs à la diable, devilled eggs
oeufs à la neige, whipped, sweetened egg whites served in a
    vanilla custard sauce (means "eggs in the snow")
oeufs au lait, egg custard
oeuf sauté à la poêle, fried egg
oeufs au vin, eggs poached in red wine
oeufs d'alose, cooked fish (shad) eggs
oeufs en meurette, poached eggs w/red wine sauce from
    Bourgogne
oeufs fermier, eggs from poultry raised on a farm
oeufs pochés suzettes, poached eggs in baked potatoes
oeuf sur la plat, fried egg
offert, free ("offered")
oie, goose
oie à l'instar de visé, goose boiled &
    then fried. A Belgian specialty
oignon, onion
oignons grelots, small pickled onions
oiseau, bird
olives, olives
olives farcies, stuffed olives
olives noires, black olives

Oie.

OiseaU~
waZoe

olives vertes, green olives
omble-chevalier, freshwater fish of the trout family (char)
omelette, omelet
omelette au fromage, cheese omelet
omelette au jambon, ham omelet
omelette au lard, bacon omelet
omelette au naturel, plain omelet
omelette aux champignons, mushroom omelet
omelette aux fines herbs, omelet w/herbs
omelette brayaude, potato omelet
omelette César, omelet w/garlic & herbs
omelette complète, omelet w/ham & cheese
omelette fourée aux pommes dite à la Normande, apple
   upside-down cake
omelette landaise, omelet w/pine nuts
omelette nature, plain omelet
omelette norvégienne, baked Alaska
omelette parmentier, potato omelet
omelette paysanne, omelet w/bacon & potatoes
omelette quercynoise, cheese & walnut omelet
onglet, hanger steak
opéra, layered spongecake w/chocolate sauce
orange, orange
orange givrée, orange sorbet served in an orange
orange pressée, fresh, squeezed orange juice
oranges en rondelles, candied orange slices in orange jelly
oreilles, ears
oreillettes, pastry puffs
orge, barley
orgeat, almond-sugar syrup
origon, oregano
orties, nettles
ortolan, small game bird
os, bone
os à moelle, marrow bone
oseille, sorrel
ostendaise, w/shrimp & oysters
ou, or
ouassous, large crayfish found in the French West Indies
oursin, sea urchin
pacanes, pecans (in Guadeloupe)

Olives Farcies.

Ortolans are eaten whole, everything but the beak. They're illegal to serve.

paëlla, saffron-flavored rice & various ingredients. There are
   many variations of this famous Spanish dish found on
   menus all over France

pagre commun, sea bream

paillard, thin, flattened piece of meat, poultry or fish fillet

pailles pommes, fried, shredded potatoes

paillettes, cheese straws

pain, bread

pain au chocolat, chocolate-filled pastry

pain au lait, sweet bun

pain aux noix, walnut bread

pain aux raisins, bun w/custard & white raisins

pain blanc, white bread

pain complet, whole-wheat bread

pain de campagne, chewy "country" bread

pain de mie, sliced white bread (sandwich bread)

pain d'épices, gingerbread/a dense spice cake w/honey

pain de seigle, rye bread

pain de son, bran bread

pain de sucre, sugar loaf

pain grillé, toast

pain noir, dark bread

pain ordinaire, French bread

pain perdu, French toast. Literally,
   "lost bread" invented because French bread has no
   preservatives, thus becomes hard very quickly.
   The milk & eggs soften the bread

pain viennois, Vienna loaf

palaia, small sardines & anchovies

palais, cookies. *Palais de dames* are fruit cookies

paleron, shoulder of beef

paletot, skin, bone & meat of a fattened goose or duck (after the
   liver is removed)

palets de marrons, puréed-chestnut patties

palette de porc, pork shoulder

palmiers, palm hearts (*coeurs de palmier*). This can also refer to
   a caramelized puff pastry

paloise, *béarnaise* sauce w/mint

palombe, pigeon

palourdes, clams

pamplemousse, grapefruit

Pain ~
Pan

*Bread is
buttered at
breakfast but
not lunch or
dinner.*

*Always liked
that word.*

panaché, mixed. *Un panaché* also refers to a drink made of half beer and half lemon soda

panade, thick mixture used to bind dumplings (panada)

panais, parsnip

pan bagnat, large round sandwich filled w/olive oil, onions, olives, tomatoes, anchovies & a hard-boiled egg. A specialty on the Côte d'Azur (means "wet bread"). This is a *salade niçoise* sandwich

pané, breaded

panier, basket

panisses, chickpea-flour pancake (deep fried)

panne de porc, fat from the kidneys of a pig

pannequet, rolled, filled crêpe

papalines, orange-flavored chocolates from Avignon

papeton d'aubergines, eggplant casserole from Avignon (means "eggplant of the popes")

papillons, butterfly cookies. This can also refer to a type of oyster

papillote, en, baked in parchment paper

paquets, en, in packages or parcels

parfait, ice-cream dessert. Can also refer to goose, duck or chicken-liver mousse

parfum, flavor

Paris-Brest, ring-shaped *éclair* filled w/praline cream

parisienne, a vegetable garnish w/potatoes sautéed in butter w/a white sauce

parme, amberjack (in Provence)

parmentier, dish containing potatoes

part, portion

partager, to share

passe-pierre, seaweed

Passe-Tout-Grain, red wine from Burgundy

pasta, pasta. Originally from neighboring Italy, pasta is an important part of Provençal cuisine

Pastèque.

pastèque, watermelon

pastilles, hard, fruit- or mint-flavored candy

pastis, anise-flavored aperitif. This is a Provençal word meaning mixture. It is a summer drink. Common brands are Pastis 51, Pernod, Ricard, Granier, Prado & Henri Bardouin

pastis landais, a sweet bread dessert

patate, sweet potato

patate douce, sweet potato

pâte, pastry dough.
> This can also mean a batter or paste.
> Do not confuse this w/*pâté* or *pâtes*

pâte à choux, cream-puff pastry

pâte à foncer, shortbread crust

pâte à frire, sweet french-frying batter

pâte à pain, bread dough

pâte brisée, pie pastry

pâte d'amandes, marzipan

pâte de fruits, fruit-paste candies

pâte feuilletée, puff pastry

pâte levée, bread dough

pâte sablée, sweet pie pastry

pâte sucrée, sweet pie pastry

pâté, pâté

pâté ardennais, purée of pork in a loaf of bread

pâté de campagne, *pâté* w/a variety of meats

pâté de canard, duck *pâté*

pâté de foie de volaille, chicken-liver *pâté*

pâté de foie d'oie, *pâté* that contains at least 50% goose liver & up to 50% other meats

pâté de foie gras, goose-liver *pâté*. Contains at least 75% goose liver

pâté doré, seasoned baked pork-liver *pâté* served cold

pâté en croûte, *pâté* in a pastry crust

pâté en pot, mutton soup found in the French West Indies

pâté maison et rillettes, a slice of a loaf of ground seasoned meat

pâtes, pasta

pâtisserie, pastry

patte, foot (paw) or leg of an animal or bird

patte blanche, small crayfish

patte rouge, large crayfish

Pauillac, rich red wine from Bordeaux

paupiette, slice of veal or beef rolled around stuffing

pavé, thick slice of beef (or calf's liver)

pavé aux marrons, chestnut & chocolate cake

pavot, graines de, poppy seeds

Pâte is pastry.
Pâté is pâté.
Pâtes is pasta.

Patte blanche

paysanne, à la, "country style" usually means a
    dish containing assorted vegetables
pays d'auge, cream & cider sauce
pays, du, from the area
peau, skin
pêche, peach
pêche melba, peaches w/ice cream & raspberry sauce
pêcheur, this term refers to fish preparations (means
    "fisherman")
pelardons, goat cheese
pelé, peeled
pelure, peelings
perce-pierre, seaweed
perche, perch
perdreau, young partridge
perdrix, partridge
périgourdine, à la, w/goose- or duck-liver purée & truffles
périgueux, a brown sauce w/chopped truffles
Pernod, anise-flavored aperitif
perroquet, a drink of *pastis* & mint
persil, parsley. *Persillé* means parslied
persillade, chopped parsley & garlic
pesto, see *pistou*
pétillant, slightly sparkling beverage
petit, small
petit beurre, tea biscuit
petit déjeuner, breakfast
petite friture, fried whitebait
petit four, small fancy cookie or cake
petit gâteau, small cake/cookie
petit-gris, small snail
petit noir, black coffee
petit pain, roll. *Petits pains au maïs* are made w/corn meal
petit pois, pea
petit pois de cérons, peas w/pork
petit salé, salt pork
petits farcis provençaux, stuffed vegetables of Provence
petits gâteaux, cookies
petits pois, peas
petits pois à la Normande, creamed peas
petit-suisse, creamy, unsalted cheese/cheese *beignets*

pétoncle, tiny scallop
pets de nonne, small fried pastry
pibale, small eel
pichet, pitcher of wine
picodon, goat's-milk cheese from Provence
picon bière, beer mixed w/a sweet liqueur
pièce, piece/each
pied, foot
pied de cochon, pig's foot
pied de mouton, wild mushroom/sheep's foot
pied de porc, pig's foot
pieps et paquets, stuffed-tripe dish
pietra, chestnut-flavored beer from Corsica
pieuvre, octopus
pigeon, pigeon
pigeonneau, young pigeon
pignatelle, small cheese fritter
pignons, pine nuts/croissant w/pine nuts
pilaf/pilau, rice cooked w/broth & onions
piment, chili pepper/pimento
piment doux, sweet pepper
piment en poudre, chili powder
piment poivre de Jamaïque, allspice
pimprenelle, burnet (a green used in salads)
pince, claw
pineau, cognac & grape juice
pintade, guinea hen
pintadeau, young guinea hen
pipérade, omelet w/ham, green peppers, tomatoes & garlic
piquant, spicy hot
piquante, sauce of pickles or capers, shallots & vinegar
piqué, larded
pissala, fish purée used in *pissaladière*
pissaladière, pizza-like tart w/onions,
    black olives & purée of anchovies
    & sardines (from Provence)
pissenlit, dandelion leaves
pistache, pistachio
pistil de safran, thread of saffron
pistou, garlic, basil, nuts & olive oil sauce (known as pesto in
    Italy)/pesto soup

pichet.

pee-shay

Piment doux

Never warmed
up to this

pithiviers, puff pastry filled w/ground almonds & sweet cream

pizza, pizza is not shared in France, is not eaten w/your hands & will be served w/a bottle of olive oil w/hot peppers at the bottom. The oil is to spice up your pizza. A cheese & tomato pizza is called a ***marguerite***

pizza quatres saisons, four-seasons pizza (four toppings: ham, mushrooms, cheese & anchovy)

pizza reine, pizza topped w/ham & mushrooms

planteurs, rum & fruit punches found in the French West Indies

plaque de chocolat, chocolate bar

plat, plate/dish

plat de résistance, main course

plat du jour, plate (special) of the day

plate, flat-shelled oyster. This can also refer to water w/out carbonation

plateau, platter

plateau de fromages, platter of cheeses. In Normandy, this is almost always served w/*calvados*

plat froid, cold plate

plat minceur, diet plate

plat principal (plats principaux), main course(s)

pleurote, grey mushroom found in the Loire Valley

plie, flounder/plaice

plie franche, flounder

plombières, vanilla ice-cream dessert w/whipped cream & candied fruit

pluviers, plovers (small birds)

poché, poached

pochouse, fish & onion stew prepared w/wine (from Bourgogne)

poêle, à la, fried

point, à, medium done. In France, this means still pink

pointe, tip. *Pointe d'asperge* is an asparagus tip

poire, pear

poireau (poireaux), leek(s)

poire Belle Hélène, pear w/ice cream & chocolate sauce

poirier d'anjou, pear cake

Plat minceur. I hope you're just looking this up to see what it is, not ordering it!

Plie.

A poêle is a frying pan.

pois, peas

pois chiche, chick-pea

pois mange-tout, snow pea

poisson, fish

poisson à grande friture, deep-dried fish

poisson d'eau douce, freshwater fish

poisson de mer, saltwater fish

poissonnerie, fish soup/fish store

poitrine, breast

poitrine d'agneau Sainte Menehould, braised & grilled
lamb breast

poitrine demi-sel, slab of unsmoked bacon

poitrine de mouton, mutton breast

poitrine de porc, pork belly

poitrine de veau, veal breast

poitrine fumée, slab of smoked bacon

poivrade, brown sauce of wine, vegetables, peppers & vinegar

poivre, pepper. *Au poivre* means w/peppercorns

poivre d'Ain, flavored *banon* (cheese)

poivre d'ane, bitter, peppery herb

poivre de cayenne, very hot red pepper

poivre de Chine, mouth-numbing type of peppercorn

poivre de la Jamaïque, allspice (the main ingredient of jerk
seasoning)

poivre frais de Madagascar, green peppercorns

poivre mignonette, crushed peppercorns used on steaks

poivre noir, black peppercorns

poivre rose, pink peppercorns

poivre vert, green peppercorns

poivron, bell pepper

poivron doux, sweet bell pepper

poivron épicé, hot pepper

poivron rouge, red pepper

poivron vert, green pepper

polenta, corn meal/polenta (dish of
boiled corn meal, w/butter & cheese)

Pomerol, a red wine (merlot) from Bordeaux

pommade, a thick paste

pomme, apple

pomme au four, potato baked in its skin

pomme bonne femme, baked apple

poisson.

*au four
litchally
"in the oven"*

pomme de terre, potato

pomme de terre brayaude, oven-cooked potato

pomme en l'air, caramelized apple slices
    served w/blood sausage

pommes à l'anglaise, boiled potatoes

pommes allumettes, very thin french fries

pommes anna, sliced potato & cheese dish

pommes boulangère, a potato &
    meat dish/sliced potatoes w/onions

pommes château, potatoes fried in butter

pommes dauphine, potatoes mashed in
    butter & egg yolks, mixed in flour
    & deep fried

Most of the time pomme refers to potato though it means apple... sorry can't be more specific.

pommes dauphinoise, potatoes baked w/garlic, cheese & milk

pommes de terre à la berrichonne, herbed potatoes

pommes de terre à l'angoumois, potato & cabbage casserole

pommes duchesse, potatoes mashed in butter & egg yolks

pommes en robe de chambre, potatoes in their skin

pommes en robe des champs, potatoes in their skin

pommes fondantes, potatoes cooked in butter

pommes frites, french fries

pommes gratinées, potatoes baked w/cheese

pommes lyonnaises, potatoes sautéed w/onions

pommes mousseline, mashed potatoes

pommes nature, boiled or steamed potatoes

pommes nouvelles, new potatoes

pommes paille, fried strips of potatoes

pommes Pont-Neuf, french fries

Pommes frites, one of the miraculous joys of France.

pommes renversées, baked caramelized apple pudding

pommes sautées, fried potatoes

pommes soufflées, puffy slices of potatoes fried twice

pommes vapeur, steamed or boiled potatoes

pompe à l'huile, sweet flat bread flavored w/olive oil

pont l'évêque, strong, flavored, semi-hard cheese (usually
    served in square blocks)

porc, pork

porc au lait, pork cooked in milk

porc aux deux pommes, pork w/potatoes & apples

porc demi-sel, salted pork

porcelet, young suckling pig

porchetta/porketta, an Italian dish of roast, stuffed suckling pig

porc salé, salted pork

Porto, port

porto, au, w/port

port-salut/port du salut, mild, soft, buttery cheese

portugaises, a type of oyster

potable, drinkable

potage, soup (usually thick)

potage à la crème de coco, cream-of-coconut soup found in the French West Indies

potage au cerfeuil, soup of chervil & other herbs. A specialty in the Ardennes region of Belgium

potage bilbi, fish & oyster soup

potage bonne femme, potato & leek soup

potage cancalais, fish soup

potage Crécy, carrot soup

potage crème normande, cream of fish soup

potage cressonière, watercress soup

potage cultivateur, soup w/mixed vegetables & pork

potage d'Auvergne, lentil & potato soup

potage du Père Tranquille, lettuce soup

potage du Barry, cauliflower soup

potage Longchamp, soup featuring peas

potage nivernaise, carrot soup

potage parmentier, leek & potato soup

potage portugais, tomato *potage*

potage printanier, vegetable soup

potage Saint-Germain, split-pea soup

potage soissonnais, haricot-bean soup

potage velouté, creamy soup

pot-au-feu, stew of meat & vegetables

pot-de-crème, mousse or custard dessert

potée, boiled pork (or beef) w/cabbage

pothine de boeuf, beef braised w/*calvados*. The *pothine* is a cast-iron casserole in which this dish is cooked

potiron, pumpkin

Pouilly-Fuissé, dry white wine from Burgundy

poularde, capon/fatted chicken

poularde Sainte-Hélène, chicken w/dumplings

poule, hen

poule au pot, stewed chicken w/vegetables

poule au riz, hen served w/rice

potage.

poule d'Inde, turkey hen

poule faisane, pheasant

poule farcie en daube à la berrichonne, boned, stuffed chicken in jelly.

NOT crazy about jellied meat.

poulet, chicken

poulet basquaise, chicken w/sweet peppers & tomatoes ("Basque style")

poulet Biarritz, chicken in white wine

poulet chasseur, chicken usually w/mushrooms & white wine. This can also be chicken in tomato sauce

poulet.

poulet créole, chicken in a white sauce (often spicy) & served w/rice

poulet de Bresse, free-range, corn-fed chicken

poulet de grain, corn-fed chicken. Sold in shops with a special ring around its "foot" to prove they are authentic.

poulet de Saint-Astier, chicken stew

poulet fermier, free-range chicken

poulet Marengo, chicken cooked in white wine w/tomatoes, garlic, mushrooms & shallots. Said to be the chicken dish served to Napoleon after the battle of Marengo in 1800

poulet rôti, roast chicken

poulpe, octopus

pourboire, tip

poulpe.

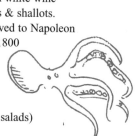

pour/à emporter, to go/take out

pourpier, purslane (a green used in salads)

pousse-pierre, seaweed

poussin, spring chicken

praire, clam

praline, caramelized almonds

premier cru, denotes a high-quality wine

pré-salé, lambs that graze on salt meadows

pressé, fresh squeezed

presse, à la, pressed

pression, draft beer.
À la pression means from the tap

primeur, early season or spring fruits & vegetables

Prince-de-Galles, stuffed w/*pâté*

printanière, à la, w/spring vegetables

prisuttu, cured ham from Corsica

prix, price

prix fixe, fixed price

prix net, service is included

profiteroles, little cream puffs filled w/ice
cream & covered in chocolate sauce

Profiteroles ~ food of the gods.

provençale, à la, w/garlic, onions, herbs & tomatoes
("Provence style"). Provence is one of
France's wine-growing regions and, of course,
one of the world's best-known &
loved tourist destinations

prune, plum

pruneau/pruneau sec, prune

pudding, custard/pudding

puits d'amour, pastry filled w/custard

pulenta, chestnut-flour bread from Corsica

purée, strained fruit or vegetables.
En purée means mashed

purée de pommes de terre, mashed potatoes

pyramide au chocolat, chocolate pyramid filled w/chocolate
pieces & sauces, whipped cream & butter

quartiers d'orange glacés, caramelized orange sections. A
dessert found on menus in Provence

quart, un, on a menu this denotes a quarter-liter of wine

quatre-épices, a blend of four spices
(nutmeg, cloves, ginger &
white pepper)

quatre-quarts, a cake made from
four ingredients – eggs, flour,
butter & sugar – of equal weight.
A specialty in Brittany

quatre-quarts is like pound cake.

quenelle, dumpling

quenelles de foie de veau, calf's-liver dumplings. A specialty in
Luxembourg

quetsche, small plum/liquor made from plums

queue, tail

queue de boeuf, oxtail

quiche, egg tart w/vegetable, seafood or meat filling

quiche au fromage blanc, bacon & white cheese *quiche*

quiche lorraine, *quiche* w/cheese, bacon & onions

râble, loin of rabbit

râble de lièvre, saddle of rabbit

racasse, scorpion fish

raclette, cheese heated until it begins to melt. The melted part is scraped off & placed on a warm plate to be eaten w/boiled potatoes, pickles & pickled onions. This can also refer to melted cheese on a *baguette*

radis, radish

radis.

radis noir, large black radish

ragoût, stewed/meat stew

raie, ray/skate (fish)

raifort, horseradish

raisin, grape(s)

raisins de Corinthe, currants

raisins.

raisins de table, dessert grapes

raisin sec, raisin(s)

raïto, red wine, tomato & onion sauce

ramequin, small cheese tart or a small casserole

rancio, dessert wine

râpé, shredded/grated. *La râpée* is a creamed-potato pancake

rascasse, fish found in the Mediterranean (scorpion fish)

ratatouille, eggplant casserole

rave, root vegetable

ravigote, vinegar dressing (w/herbs & shallots)

ravioli, ravioli. Common in Nice & all of the French Riviera

reblochon, soft, strong cheese

refroidi, chilled

*à la reine...
of the
queen.*

régional(e), from the region/local

reine, à la, w/mince meat or poultry

reine-claude, small green or yellow plums (greengage)

reinette, fall & winter apple

religieuse, *éclair* pastry. This pastry got its name because it looks like a nun in her habit

rémoulade, mayonnaise sauce

renversée, turned out of its cooking container

repas, meal

Rhône, this valley is one of France's wine regions (located in South Central France) & known for its white and red wines

rhubarbe, rhubarb

rhum, rum

Ricard, anise-flavored aperitif

Richelieu, à la, w/tomatoes, bacon & potatoes

rigotte, goat cheese

rillettes, highly seasoned meat baked in its own fat (potted meat)

rillons, pork belly
ris, sweetbreads
ris d'agneau, lamb sweetbreads
ris de..., sweetbreads
ris de veau, veal sweetbreads (the pancreas of a veal calf)
rissole, pastry/meat or fish patty
rissolé, fried until brown & crisp
riz, rice. *Crème de riz* is rice flour
    (very finely gound rice)
riz à l'impératrice, rice pudding
riz basquais, spicy rice
riz complet, brown rice
rizotto, risotto
riz pilaf, rice boiled in bouillon w/onions (rice pilaf)
riz safrané, saffron rice
riz sauvage, wild rice
robe des champs, en, in its skin
Robert, a brown sauce w/onions, white wine & mustard
rocambole, a member of the onion family
rognon, kidney
rognonnade, veal loin
rognons blancs, testicles
rognons de veau à la liégeoise, roast veal kidneys
romarin, rosemary
romsteck, rump steak
rondelle, round slice
roquefort, blue cheese
roquette, arugula (rocket)
rosbif, roast beef
rosé, rosé. This can also refer to rare meat
rosette, dried sausage/small round piece
Rossini, a dish that includes *foie gras* & truffles
rôti, roast/roasted
rouelle, a slice cut at an angle
rouelle de veau, veal shank
rouge, red
rouget, red mullet
rouille, spicy sauce of peppers, garlic & tomatoes
rouilleuse, red garlic mayonnaise
roulade, rolled slice of meat or fish w/stuffing/"Swiss roll"
    dessert w/cream or jam stuffing

Handwritten annotations:
ris - ree
riz - ree
Don't get
'em mixed
up.

Rognon ~
runyun

Pass on the
entire Rongum
selection

Rouget.

roulé, rolled

rouleau, roll of...

roussillonnade, grilled sausage & mushroom dish

roux, flour & butter mixture (used to thicken sauces or soup)

rouzoles, crêpes filled w/bacon & ham

rumsteck, rump steak

sabayon, creamy dessert of wine, sugar, egg yolks & flavoring/cream wine sauce

sablé, shortbread cookie

saccharine, saccharin

sachet de thé, tea bag

safran, saffron

saignant, very rare

saindoux, pork fat

Saint-Amour, red wine from Beaujolais

Saint-Emilion, red wine form Bordeaux

Saint-Estèphe, red wine from Bordeaux

Saint-Germain, w/peas

Saint-Honoré, cake w/cream

Saint-Hubert, sauce w/bacon & chestnuts

Saint-Jacques, sea scallop

Saint-Julien, red wine from Bordeaux

Saint-Marcellin, goats' or cows' cheese w/a smoky flavor

Saint-Raphaël, quinine-flavored aperitif

Saint-Paulin, mild, semi-soft cheese

Saint-Pierre, John Dory fish (a firm-textured, white-fleshed fish w/a mild, sweet flavor and low fat content)

saison, season

salade, salad

salade antiboise, salad usually w/fish, capers & green peppers

salade au bleu, salad w/blue cheese (& frequently walnuts)

salade au chapon, salad served on toast rubbed w/garlic

salade aux noix, green salad w/walnuts

salade cauchoise, ham, potato & celery salad

salade chiffonnade, shredded lettuce & sorrel

salade composée, chef's salad

salade d'Auvergne, salad w/blue cheese dressing

salade de boulghour, bulgur wheat salad

salade de crudités, chopped vegetable salad

salade de fruits, fruit cocktail

salade de gésiers, green salad w/gizzards

St. Emilion~ personal favorite.

Chapon refers to the toast.

salade de liège, bean & potato salad. A specialty in Belgium

salade de museau de boeuf, marinated beef headcheese

salade de saison, seasonal salad

salade de tomates, tomato salad

salade folle, mixed salad usually
  w/green beans

*Salade folle ~
crazy salad*

salade lyonnaise, *hors d'oeuvre* of seasoned meats in an oil,
  shallot & vinegar dressing

salade mélangée, mixed salad

salade mêlée, mixed salad

salade mesclun, mixed greens

salade mixte, mixed salad

salade multicolore, salad w/radishes, peppers, egg, cucumber,
  corn & basil

salade niçoise, salad usually w/tomatoes, anchovies or tuna,
  potatoes, vinegar & black olives (served as a main course)

salade panachée, mixed salad

salade paysanne, salad w/eggs & pieces of bacon

salade russe, diced vegetables in mayonnaise

salade simple, green salad

salade verte, green salad

salade wallonie, warm salad w/lettuce, bacon
  & fried potatoes. A specialty in Belgium

salaisons, an hors d'oeuvre of olives, anchovies &/or herring

salé, salted

salicorne, algae used as a condiment

salmis, roasted game or poultry

salpicon, stuffing w/sauce

*Salpicon —
like the word
and the
concept!*

salsifis, salsify (oyster plant)

Sancerre, white & pale, light-bodied red wines from the
  Loire Valley

sandre, pike

sandwich, sandwich

sandwich au fromage, cheese sandwich

sandwich au jambon, ham sandwich

sandwich au saucisson, dried-sausage sandwich

sandwich aux rillettes, *pâté* sandwich

sandwich crudités, lettuce &/or chopped
  vegetable sandwich

sang, blood

sanglier, wild boar

*Sanglier.
A specialty in
the Ardennes.*

sans, without
sans arêtes, boneless
sans peau, skinless
sarcelle, teal (river duck)
sardine, sardine
sarrasin, buckwheat
sarriette, summer savory (an herb)
sartando, small fried fish w/hot vinegar
sartenais, hard, strong cheese from Corsica
sauce, sauce/gravy/salad dressing
sauce à la crème, cream sauce
sauce aurore, a white sauce w/tomato purée
sauce aux câpres, a white sauce w/capers
sauce bigarade, orange sauce
sauce bretonne, egg, butter & mustard sauce
sauce café de Paris, cream, mustard & herb sauce
sauce catalane, tomato, orange & garlic sauce
sauce gaillarde, seasoned mayonnaise
sauce mornay, cheese sauce
sauce poulette, mushroom, egg yolk & wine sauce
sauce soubise, onion sauce
sauce Suzette, orange sauce
sauce veloutée, creamy soup/white sauce (*roux* mixed w/poultry,
   fish, veal or mushroom stock)
sauce vinot, wine sauce
saucisse, sausage
saucisse à l'ail tiède, garlic sausage
   (served warm)
saucisse à la navarraise, sausage w/wine
   & sweet peppers
saucisse de Francfort, hot dog/frankfurter
saucisse de Strasbourg, beef sausage
saucisse de Toulouse, fresh pork sausage
saucisson, dried sausage
saucisson à l'alsacienne, poached sausage w/horseradish sauce
saucisson à la lyonnaise, poached sausage w/potato salad
saucisson chaud de Lyon en croûte, red sausage w/cubes of
   fat & baked in pastry
saucisson de Lyon, dried seasoned sausage
sauge, sage
saumon, salmon

[handwritten margin notes:]
Saucisse~
Sausage like
bratwurst
Saucisson~
Sausage like
Salami

Sauge.

113

saumon de l'Atlantique, Atlantic salmon

saumon fumé, smoked salmon

Saumur-Champigny, light-bodied red wine from the
Loire Valley

saupiquet, spicy cream sauce w/bread crumbs

saupiquet des amognes, ham w/spicy cream sauce

sauté, sautéed

Sauternes, a fruity white dessert wine

sauvage, wild

Sauvignon de Touraine, white wine from the
Sauvignon Blanc grape

savarin, spongecake topped w/rum & cream

Savoie, one of France's wine-growing regions

savoyarde, flavored w/cheese. *À la savoyarde* also can refer to
a vermouth & cream sauce

scampi, prawns

scarole, escarole, a salad green (a type of *endive*)

scotch, scotch

sec, dry/straight

séché, dried

seiche, large squid/cuttlefish

seiches farcies, cuttlefish stuffed w/a mixture of sausage
& the meat of cuttlefish tentacles

seigle, rye

sel, salt

sel-épicé, salt spiced w/basil, nutmeg, cloves, cinnamon,
peppercorns, bay leaves & coriander

sel gemme, rock salt

sel gris, coarse rock or sea salt

selle, saddle of meat, generally the loin roast

selle anglaise, saddle of meat

sel marin, sea salt

selon arrivage, on a menu, this means the dish
depends on availability

selon grandeur/selon grosseur, price paid by the size or weight

sel raffiné, refined salt

semoule, semolina flour

sériole, amber jack, a type of fish

serpolet, wild thyme

serran, perch

service compris, service included

service non compris, service not include

serviette, napkin

s.g., abbreviation for price paid by the size or weight

sherry, sherry

sirop, syrup

sirop de sucre d'érable, maple syrup

smitane, cream, wine & onion sauce

socca, *crêpe* made w/chickpea flour served on the Côte d'Azur

soissons, white beans

soja, soy

sole, sole

sole normande, sole in a butter, onion, mushroom, white wine, cream & *calvados* sauce

son, bran

Sorbet.

sorbet, sherbet

soubise, onion sauce

soubise-aurore, onion & tomato sauce

soucoupe, saucer

soufflé, soufflé (beaten egg whites w/various ingredients baked in a mold)

soufflé à la reine, soufflé w/poultry or meat

soufflé au Grand Marnier, soufflé w/orange liqueur

soufflé Rothschild, vanilla-flavored fruit soufflé

soupe, soup

soupe à l'oignon gratinée, French onion soup

soupe au pistou, vegetable & noodle soup (soup w/pesto found in the South of France)

soupe corse, Corsican soup of vegetables & herbs simmered w/a ham bone

soupe de montagne, Corsican soup of vegetables & herbs simmered w/a ham bone

soupe de poisson, fish soup

soupe paysanne, Corsican soup of vegetables & herbs simmered w/a ham bone

soupe pêcheur, fish soup

spaghetti, spaghetti

spats, small fish of the herring family

spécialité, specialty

spécialité de la maison, house specialty

spécialité du chef, chef's specialty

spécialités locales, local dishes

steak, steak

steak au poivre, steak topped w/crushed peppercorns. ***Steak au poivre vert*** is steak in a green-peppercorn sauce & ***steak au poivre rouge*** is steak in a red-peppercorn sauce

steak frites, steak & french fries

steak haché, hamburger

steak tartare, raw hamburger or chopped beef (usually topped w/a raw egg)

stockfish, niçoise spicy fish stew

stufatu, Corsican stew w/pasta

succès au pralin, meringue cake w/almonds

sucettes, lollipops ("suckers")

suchi, sushi

sucre, sugar

sucre candi, candy sugar

sucre de canne roux, brown sugar

sucre filé, spun sugar

Sucre filé is found adorning Croquembouche.

suprême, chicken-based sauce/breast of chicken or game or fillet of fish w/an unusual combination of ingredients

suprême de volaille, chicken breast. Usually a boned chicken breast in a creamy sauce

sur commande, to your special order

surgelé(s), frozen food

surlonge, beef chuck roast

sus, en, in addition. ***Boisson en sus*** means drink not included

Suze, an aperitif flavored w/gentian, an herb

tablier de sapeur, grilled breaded tripe

tagine/tajine, stew (lamb, veal or chicken) w/vegetables. This spicy stew is a specialty in North Africa (especially Morocco). Also a clay cooking vessel

Tagine.

tanche, the freshwater fish tench

tapenade, mixture of black olives, olive oil, lemon juice, capers & anchovies (a spread from Provence)

Tanche.

tarama, mullet-roe spread

tartare, chopped raw beef/in a salad, this refers to a mayonnaise-based sauce

tarte, pie/tart

tarte à l'oignon, onion & cream tart

tarte alsacienne, apple & custard tart

tarte au citron meringuée, lemon meringue pie

tarte au fruit, fruit tart

tartelette, small tart

tarte tatin, upside-down apple tart. Legend has it that this tart was "created" when the Tatin sisters (who operated a restaurant) put the tart in the oven & left for church. They discovered their mistake, turned it upside down & served it.

tarte tropézienne, yellow cake w/custard filling (created by a Polish baker in 1955 in St Tropez)

tartine, open-faced sandwich (half baguette w/butter)

tasse, cup

Tavel, rosé wine from the Côte du Rhône region

tendre, tender

tendre de tranche, round steak

tendron, breast

tendron de veau, veal breast

terrine, *pâté*/prepared in an earthenware dish

terrine de campagne, pork & liver *pâté*

terrine de légumes, ground & seasoned vegetable loaf

terrinée, caramel-rice pudding

tête, head

tête de veau vinaigrette, calf's head w/vinegar & oil dressing

teurgoule, caramel-rice pudding

thé, tea

thé au lait, tea w/milk

thé citron, tea w/ lemon

thé glacé, iced tea

thé nature, tea w/out milk

thon, tuna

thon mirabeau, tuna cooked in eggs & milk

thym, thyme

tian, a dish (usually rice, vegetables & cheese) cooked in an oval-shaped earthenware dish used on the Côte d'Azur

tian de Saint-Jacques et légumes provençal, sea scallops on a bed of chopped vegetables

tiède, lukewarm

tilleul, herb tea

timbale, cup. *En timbale* means meat, fish or fruit in a mold

ti punch, rum, lime & sugarcane syrup drink found in the French West Indies

The luscious-sounding Tartine buerré is Nothing more than buttered bread.

Not on your life!

Ti means petit

117

tisane, herbal tea

toast, toast (little pieces of crispy bread)

tomate, tomato. This also is the name for
a drink of *pastis* mixed w/grenadine

Tomates.

tomates à la provençal, baked tomatoes stuffed w/bread
crumbs, garlic & parsley

tomates concassées, roughly chopped tomatoes

tomates farcies, tomatoes stuffed w/seasoned bread crumbs

tomme (or tome) au marc, the crust of this smooth & creamy
cheese is made of grape pulp. Also known as *fondu aux
raisins*

tomme (de Savoie), soft, mild cheese

tonique, tonic

tonneaux en chêne, oak barrels

Tortue.

topinambour, Jerusalem artichoke

tortue, turtle

tortue véritable, turtle soup

toulousaine, usually means served w/sweetbreads or truffles
("Toulouse style")

tourain, bread & garlic soup

tourin bordelais, French onion soup (usually w/bread on the
bottom of the bowl)

tournedos, round cut of prime steak

tournedos Rossini, *tournedos* served w/Madeira wine sauce &
served w/*foie gras* &/or truffles

Tourteau.

tourta da blea, Swiss chard pie

tourte, pie

tourteau, large crab

tourte aux blettes, sweet tart of eggs,
cheese, raisins, pine nuts & chard

tourte du jour, savory pie of the day

tourtière, pastry filled w/prunes &/or apples.
Also the name for a cooking dish

tourton, pastry filled w/prunes, apples, spinach & garlic

tout compris, everything is included in the price

tout épice, allspice

tranche, slice. *Tranché* means sliced

tranche grasse, sirloin tip

tranche napolitaine, slice of layered ice cream

travers de porc, spareribs

treipen, black pudding & sausages w/potatoes

très, very

trifle, trifle

tripe, tripe

tripe à la luxembourgeoise, tripe specialty found in Luxembourg

tripes à la mode, tripe in butter, onions & *calvados*. A popular dish in Normandy

tripes à la mode de Caen, tripe baked w/calf's feet

tripes à la mode narbonnaise, tripe in tomato sauce

Triple Sec, orange liqueur

tripoux, mutton tripe

trompettes des morts, wild mushrooms

tronçon, large slice of meat or fish

trouchia, trout. In Provence, this refers to an omelet

truffat, potato-cream pie

truffe, truffle. *Truffé* means w/truffles. Truffles are extremely expensive wild fungi that grow around the roots of trees. They must be "sniffed out" by pigs or dogs. *Truffes* also refers to chocolate truffles

truffettes dauphinoise, chocolate truffles

truite, trout

truite à l'ardennaise, Belgian dish of trout cooked in a wine sauce

truite au bleu, poached trout

truite meunière, trout in a parsley & butter sauce

truite saumonée, salmon trout

ttoro, Basque mixed-fish dish

tuile, almond cookie

turbon, ingredients cooked in a ring mold

turbot, turbot, a fish

turbotin, small turbot

vacherin, mellow Swiss cheese

vacherin glacée, baked meringue dessert

valençay, goat's-milk cheese

Vallée d'Ange, w/cooked apples & cream (named after a region in Normandy)

vanille, vanilla

vanneau, small bird

vapeur, steamed

varié/variés, assorted

veau, veal

handwritten note: Remember the general rule about Tripe... don't.

handwritten label: Truite.

veau Marengo, veal w/garlic, tomatoes, white wine & cognac

végétarien/végétarienne, vegetarian

velouté, creamy soup/white sauce
    (*roux* mixed w/poultry, fish,
      veal or mushroom stock)

velouté d'asperges, creamy white asparagus soup

venaison, venison

ventre, stomach/belly

ventrèche, salted & seasoned pork belly

vénus, clam

verdures, green salad vegetables

verjus, the juice of unripened grapes

vermicelle, tiny, thin noodles used in soup

vermouth, vermouth

vernis, large clam

verre, glass

vert, green/a sauce of spinach,
    mayonnaise & herbs

vert-pré, watercress garnish

verveine, the herbal tea lemon verbena

vessie, cooked in a pig's bladder

viande, meat

viande séchée, thin slices of cured beef

viandes froides, cold meats

vichy, w/glazed carrots

vichyssoise, cold leek & potato soup

vieille, old

vieille cure, wine-distilled liqueur

vieille prune, plum-based *eau-de-vie*

vierge beurre, a simple butter sauce w/lemon juice, salt & pepper

vierge huile d'olive, virgin olive oil

vieux, old

vigneronne, sauce w/grapes & wine

vigne, sarments de, vine cuttings used w/grilled foods

vin, wine

vinaigre, vinegar

vinaigre balsamique, balsamic vinegar

vinaigre de vin, wine vinegar

vinaigrette, generally a salad dressing
    of vinegar, mustard, herbs & oil

vin blanc, white wine

Handwritten notes:

Verjus is sometimes used instead of vinegar.

Une verre de vin rouge

Vielle cure means remedy... An excuse to drink...

Vin is pronounced Van with just a hint of the 'N'.

vin chambré, wine served at room temperature

vin cuit, sweet dessert wine

Vin Délimité de Qualité Supérieure (VDQS), denotes a local
wine made according to strict standards

vin de maison, house wine

vin de paille, straw wine w/a strong flavor & aroma

vin de pays, wine guaranteed to originate in a certain region
("country wine")

vin de table, table wine

vin de xérès, sherry

vin doux, sweet wine/dessert wine

vin doux naturel, naturally sweet wine

vin du pays, local wine

vin gris, pink wine

vin jaune, yellow wine

vin liquoreux, sweet wine

vin mousseux, sparkling wine

vin nouveau, new wine

vin ordinaire, table wine

vin rosé, rosé wine

vin rouge, red wine

vin sec, dry wine

violet de Provence, braid of garlic

violette, crystallized violet petals

vivant/vivante, alive/living

vodka, vodka

volaille, poultry

*The French don't
fill their glasses
more than
halfway*

*Volaille ~
Voe-Lie.*

vol-au-vent, puff pastry filled w/fish, meat &/or sweetbreads

waterzooi, chicken or fish poached in a sauce w/vegetables. A
Belgian specialty

waterzooi de poulet, chicken poached in a sauce w/vegetables

whisky, whisky

Williamine, a pear brandy

xérès, sherry

yaourt/yogourt, yogurt

Yvorne, a dry Swiss white wine

zeste, citrus zest

zeste de citron, lemon zest

zeste de citron confits, candied lemon zest

zeste d'orange, orange zest

zewelwai, onion & cream tart from Alsace

Descriptions of restaurants listed here can be found on the page number following each listing.

THINGS CHANGE!

Phone numbers, prices, addresses, quality of food, etc. all change. If you come across any new information, we'd appreciate hearing from you. No item is too small! You can e-mail us through:

www.eatndrink.com

Books in the *Eating & Drinking on the Open Road* series are available at special discounts for bulk purchases for promotions or premiums. Special editions, including corporate imprints and personalized covers, can be created in large quantities. For more information, contact the publisher or authors.

ACKNOWLEDGMENTS

Thanks to Mme. Marie Fossier (our helpful contributor and French editor), Marian Olson (our friend and English editor), and Jonathan Stein at Open Road Publishing.

Special thanks to those who have helped us find the restaurants in this guide: Mark Berry, Evelyn Coulon, Jay Filter, Loralyn Lasoued and Dan Schmidt.

RESTAURANT AND FOOD NOTES

RESTAURANT AND FOOD NOTES

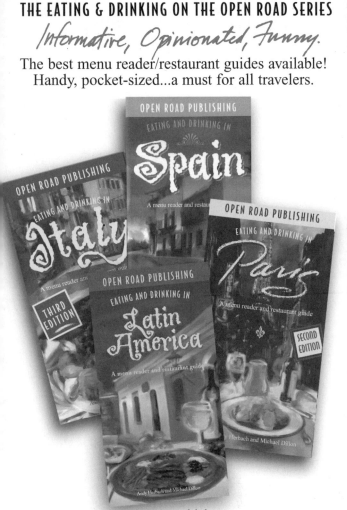